784059

CAMBODIA
Starvation
and Revolution

George Hildebrand
Gareth Porter

CAMBODIA

Starvation
and Revolution

Monthly Review Press
New York and London

Library of Congress Cataloging in Publication Data
Hildebrand, George C.
  Cambodia: starvation and revolution.
  Includes bibliographical references.
    1. Cambodia—Rural conditions. 2. Starvation. 3. Food supply—Cambodia. 4. Cambodia—History—Civil War, 1970-1975. I. Porter, Gareth, 1942-joint author. II. Title.
HN700.C32H54   320.9'596'04 76-1646
ISBN 0-85345-382-9

First printing

Monthly Review Press
62 West 14th Street, New York, N.Y. 10011
21 Theobalds Road, London WC1X 8SL

Manufactured in the United States of America

Contents

Foreword
by George McT. Kahin

Of all the American interventions in Southeast Asia, the one whose character and consequences are least known in this country is that launched against Cambodia. Because of the paucity of news coverage and the efforts by the administration to suppress much of the pertinent information, Americans have an even more distorted perception of realities in Cambodia than was the case with Vietnam or Laos. The present study is the first substantial corrective I have seen. In their documented and comprehensive account, George Hildebrand and Gareth Porter provide what is undoubtedly the best informed and clearest picture yet to emerge of the desperate economic problems brought about in Cambodia largely as a consequence of American intervention, and of the ways in which that country's new leadership has undertaken to meet them.

In assessing the situation confronted by the new Cambodian government, the authors point out that when it took power Phnom Penh's population had increased from about 600,000 to between four and five times that number, and that in the other urban centers there had also been large increases. Altogether more than a third of the country's rural population had moved to the cities to escape from the war, especially from the heavy American bombing. This enormously swollen urban population had previously been dependent for much of its food upon American airlifts and river convoys. However, these supplies had not been sufficient, and as early as September 1974 there was a significant amount of starvation in the urban centers controlled by Lon Nol's government. Moreover, the bombing and ground fighting had torn up many of the richest farming areas and reduced agricultural manpower by killing or wounding between 10 and 15 percent of the rural population. And, of course, many of the roads linking the cities and most productive areas had been destroyed or seriously damaged.

Against this background it is easier to understand the evacuation of Phnom Penh that ensued so soon after the collapse of Lon Nol's government and the ending of the American airlift. (It should be recalled that the Ford administration was unwilling to make arrangements so that the urban Cambodian population could continue to receive food.) Lacking the means to bring sufficient food into the cities, the new government decided to take the people to the food, substantial stocks of which it had stored in rural areas. These mass movements were not, then, applications of some irrational ideology, but reflected pragmatic solutions by leaders who had to rely exclusively on Cambodia's own food resources and who lacked facilities for its internal transport.

The authors follow their account of living conditions in Phnom Penh and the evacuation with what is, I believe, their major contribution. This is an extensive analysis of how in the years leading up to the National United Front's assumption of power, it managed to turn a shattered rural economy into a strong enough base from which to wage a successful war against Lon Nol's American-supported regime, and then move rapidly on to develop the extensive additional agricultural resources that enabled it to feed an urban populace nearly as large as the predominantly rural population previously under its control. The authors describe how the new government's methods of meeting these problems involved nothing less than an agricultural revolution. They show that in addition to an apparently effective social mobilization, this has involved an intensive effort to harness Cambodia's water resources that has made possible a major expansion of agricultural production through extensive double-cropping. Finally, they point out that though Cambodia's new government has thus far focused its efforts mainly on the rural areas and the need for increasing food production, it is not overlooking the cities, where industries are now being resuscitated and incorporated into a national production plan.

Anyone who is interested in understanding the situation obtaining in Phnom Penh before and after the Lon Nol government's collapse and the character and programs of the Cambodian government that has replaced it will, I am sure, be grateful to the authors of this valuable study.

—George McT. Kahin
Cornell University

Introduction

One year after the conclusion of the second Indochina war there seems little inclination in the United States to examine critically an experience that, in the words of one commentator, "stopped the 'American Century' cold in its second decade." Yet without a thorough investigation of this now historical period, Americans cannot understand this country's first overseas defeat and its future implications.

Nowhere was the war so brutal, so devoid of concern for human life, or so shattering in its impact on a society as in Cambodia. But while U.S. government and news media commentary have contrived to avoid the subject of the death and devastation caused by the U.S. intervention in Cambodia, they have gone to great lengths to paint a picture of a country ruled by irrational revolutionaries, without human feelings, determined to reduce their country to barbarism. In shifting the issue from U.S. crimes in Cambodia to the alleged crimes of the Cambodian revolutionary government, the United States has offered its own version of the end of the Cambodian war and the beginning of the new government. This study is aimed at setting the record straight on these crucial events. Although we have focused on the policies followed by the two sides toward the problem of feeding the population—an issue of fundamental importance to any society—we have also dealt with aspects of the historical drama that became intertwined with the politics of food: corruption, medical care, the U.S. bombing campaign, and the problem of economic development.

The U.S. military intervention in Cambodia was neither an aberration nor an accident. It sprang from long-standing policies of hostility toward the Vietnamese and Chinese revolutions—policies that first attempted to limit the independence Cambodia won from the French in 1953, then militated against its subsequent attempt to maintain a nonaligned policy in the Cold War, then encouraged the armed occupation of Cambodian territory by U.S.-backed right-wing regimes in neighboring Vietnam and Thailand and instigated armed subversion by dissident elements inside Cambodia.

The coup staged by General Lon Nol on March 18, 1970, and the Nixon administration's subsequent invasion were only the climax of nearly two decades of the United States' refusal to accept a truly independent Cambodia. The events of 1970 were the result of a congruence of interest between the U.S. warmakers and the Cambodian right. On one hand, the U.S. military increasingly recognized after 1967 that it could not defeat the liberation forces in South Vietnam without attacking the base areas of main-force Vietnamese units stationed along the frontier in Cambodia and Laos. At the same time, Cambodia's right-wing forces were growing increasingly powerful. The right strongly resented Prince Sihanouk's nationalization of foreign trade and his cancellation of U.S. aid, both of which directly attacked their economic interests. By 1969 the right had brought about the installation of a reactionary Premier—Lon Nol—diverted tax receipts from Prince Sihanouk's control to their own, won back international commerce for the private sector, and reestablished diplomatic relations with the United States. Prince Sihanouk, however, remained chief of state, and Cambodia not only continued to have a warm relationship with the Vietnamese but also recognized the southern liberation struggle's Provisional Revolutionary Government. In the fall of 1969, however, the Cambodian military stepped up harassment of the Vietnamese liberation forces. As Khmer Serei leader Son

Ngoc Thanh, one of the masterminds of the 1970 coup, told an American journalist in 1972, "Sihanouk had power. We wanted it. The way to get it was to attack the Vietcong."

Within forty-eight hours of the coup the United States recognized Lon Nol's regime. Within six weeks President Nixon launched the U.S. invasion of Cambodia and prepared to assume a virtually unlimited commitment to the Phnom Penh regime. Nixon did not at first intend the April 30 invasion to be restricted either in scope or duration: these limitations were announced only after the death of six American students and massive demonstrations rocked the United States. Despite this overwhelming public sentiment, the Nixon administration proceeded to adopt policies that became the five-year commitment to the Lon Nol regime. Financially, Nixon and his successor poured $1.9 billion into Lon Nol's hands. Nixon called it "the best foreign policy investment the United States has made in my lifetime." Militarily, Lon Nol's forces were trained and advised by the United States, in defiance of Congressional sanctions, while U.S. planes dropped nearly 400,000 tons of bombs on the Cambodian countryside. This entire support package was described by Nixon himself as the "Nixon Doctrine in its purest form."

Even so, the U.S. intervention was a failure. By December 1970 a report for the Senate Foreign Relations Committee found Phnom Penh already effectively isolated, while the revolutionary National United Front of Kampuchea (NUFK) claimed control of 70 percent of the country. By the summer of 1974, when Secretary of State Kissinger vetoed any U.S. contact with the NUFK on the grounds that Lon Nol was too weak to survive, Washington clearly knew the outcome. By January 1975, when the NUFK blockage choked off the Mekong River supply route from South Vietnam, the *dénouement* was even clearer.

Nevertheless, the Ford administration was determined to keep the war going. To do so it was forced to take air-cargo space reserved for foodstuffs and use it for ammunition. For Phnom Penh, swollen with refugees from the bombing of the countryside and dependent on the United States for its basic food—rice—this decision amounted to a death sentence passed on the civilian population.

Cambodia was not a passive spectator to the United States aggression. The 1970 coup found Cambodia's revolutionary left already established in the countryside and prepared to undertake a national liberation struggle while simultaneously developing the country's agricultural base. Within five days of the coup the National United Front was set up in order to confront the new situation.

The NUFK had both national tradition and recent experience to build upon in organizing the resistance. From the moment the French colonialists arrived in the 1860s there were resistance movements organized to oppose them. During the first Indochina war the Nekhum Issarak Khmer—Cambodian Liberation Front— more than half of whose cadre were patriotic monks, mounted an independence struggle in coordination with the Vietnamese and Laotians, and it occupied three-fifths of the nation's territory by the close of 1953. The Nekhum Issarak's connections with the NUFK can be seen in the adoption of its banner—a silhouette of Angkor in gold on a red field—as the official flag of the State of Democratic Kampuchea on January 5, 1976.

Then in the 1950s the Cambodian resistance formed the Pracheachon, or People's Association. It supported Prince Sihanouk's policies of peace and nonalignment but remained critical of his domestic policy. Despite many welfare and development projects, often undertaken with foreign assistance, the Khmer peasantry remained largely unaffected by Phnom Penh's programs. At the same time, the government became increasingly tainted with corruption. For young Cambodians studying at home or abroad, and for honest civil servants, radical solutions seemed to offer the only alternative.

But the time was not yet ripe. Lon Nol, at that time defense minister, carried out repressions that prevented the Pracheachon from successfully organizing for the elections mandated by the Geneva Conference of 1954. These threats against leftists continued into the 1960s, and beginning in 1963 well-known progressives began to leave Phnom Penh for the countryside. By the time of the 1970 coup, the basis for a revolutionary people's war was there.

In the face of the onslaught of U.S. power and largely isolated from the world, the Cambodian revolution adopted as a central principle the policy of *klouon opatham klouon*—self-reliance. The liberation forces boast of not having a single officer trained in either Cambodian or foreign military academies, and of having acquired more than half of their material by capturing them from "quarter-master Lon Nol."

That policy of self-reliance formed the core of the NUFK's approach to the food-short cities at the close of the war, when the people were taken to the rice-producing countryside instead of left to await the vagaries of international assistance. Today the policy of self-reliance underlies Cambodia's agricultural development, for it is the labor of the Khmer people themselves that has transformed the countryside. The impressive increases in agricultural production discussed in this book have not been brought about through the introduction of pesticides, chemical fertilizers, energy-consuming machinery, or "miracle" strains of rice. They have instead been achieved through applications of natural fertilizers and by the construction of water-raising devices adapted from bicycle parts and automobile engines. Aid has been received from friendly countries, but it has been only a minor factor in Cambodia's development.

It would hardly seem possible to discuss postwar Cambodia without solidly grounding one's analysis in the two most salient features of the country today—the enormous destruction facing it as a result of the U.S. intervention and the major advances in agricultural production brought about by the NUFK. Yet this is precisely what has occurred in most current reporting on Cambodia. In many instances U.S. government officials are directly responsible for these inaccurate interpretations; in others, their analysis has been uncritically adopted. Their motives for misrepresenting conditions seem clear: by focusing on the NUFK's alleged crime of evacuating Phnom Penh, they have been able to cover up the actual crime committed by the United States in spreading the war to Cambodia in the first place. At the same time, a substitute for the long-promised "bloodbath"—for many years the official justification for continuing the war—has been provided. Allegations of starvation were thus simply an attempt to further blacken the image of successful revolution in Indochina in the wake of the U.S. defeat.

During the war there were, of course, individual correspondents who conveyed something of the reality of the U.S. intervention. But the press was never able accurately to assess the reality of revolutionary power in Cambodia. Despite information easily obtainable in either Paris or Peking, the press entirely missed the most important development in Cambodia in six hundred years—the reintroduction of two rice crops a year, which provided the material basis for the success of the NUFK. The media did not even report Cambodia's agricultural revolution as a "claim" made by the NUFK.

Having continually discounted the NUFK and failed to appreciate the dimensions of the U.S.-induced starvation of Phnom Penh, the press was at a total loss to explain the evacuation of Cambodia's cities. Hence the widespread currency afforded official reports of starvation. Hence also the promotion of the idea that the NUFK had imposed a peasant revolution at gunpoint upon the population of Phnom Penh—a population 85 percent of whom had been forced *from* the countryside by the U.S. bombing and whose so-called urban environment had ceased to function.

Just as it neglected to draw appropriate conclusions from the inadequately reported deterioration of Phnom Penh, the press also failed to communicate the necessity for revolution in rural Cambodia. It made symbols of the fourteen-year-old peasant soldiers of the liberation army, who strode into Phnom Penh laden with bandoliers, but largely ignored the rural situations from whence they came. Yet widely available statistics indicate that their grandparents died in their fifties, exhausted by work and intestinal parasites. Far too many of their mothers died in child-birth, and most of their female relatives lived out their lives as illiterates. The majority of their elder brothers never studied beyond primary school. They themselves saw many of their generation lost to disease and debilitation. This can hardly have been the "demi-paradise" one *New York Times* columnist recently described in prewar Cambodia.

In these conditions lie the real roots of the Cambodian revolution. Here lies the explanation for the ability to prosecute the war through sixty-one terrible months, for the enormous increases in agricultural productivity, for the collective effort to overcome years of destruction and centuries of decline and to build a modern state. The story of the final phase of the war, of the country's effort to feed its people in the face of enormous odds, is one of the most dramatic episodes in the epic struggle of the peoples of that region. Sooner or later Americans must attempt to understand what happened and what has been achieved in Cambodia. We hope this study will be a useful contribution to that effort.

CAMBODIA,
WITH ZONES OF CONTROL
AS OF MAY 1974

COMPLETELY LIBERATED
ZONES

PARTIALLY LIBERATED
AND GUERRILLA ZONES

SOUTH   VIETNAM

LAOS

THAILAND

RATANAKIRI

STUNG
TRENG

MONDULKIRI

KRATIE

Stung Treng

Kratie

Mekong R.

KOMPONG
CHAM

PREAH
VIHEAR

KOMPONG THOM

Kompong Thom

Kompong
Cham

PREY
VENG

Prey Veng

SVAY
RIENG

Svay Rieng

Mekong R.

ODDAR MEAN CHEY

SIEM REAP

Angkor Wat

Siem Reap

Tonle   Sap

Tonle Sap

Kompong
Chhnang

KOMPONG
CHHNANG

Phnom Penh

Tonle Bassac

KANDAL

Takhmao

TAKEO

Takeo

Sisophon

Mongkol Borei

BATTAMBANG

Battambang

Pursat

PURSAT

KOMPONG
SPEU

Kompong Speu

Ang Tasom

KAMPOT

Kampot

KOH KONG

Sihanoukville

Ream

Gulf of
Thailand

1

The Politics of Starvation in Phnom Penh

At the time of the Lon Nol coup in 1970 Cambodia was one of the world's rice-exporting countries. Between 1970 and its final collapse in April 1975, the Lon Nol regime received a total of nearly $1.9 billion in U.S. assistance. Yet by late 1974 massive starvation was stalking Phnom Penh. How and why Cambodians starved to death in large numbers under the government of the Khmer Republic (or GKR, as the Lon Nol side was called by the U.S. government) is one of the most important aspects of the tragedy of the Cambodian war.

The starvation that afflicted Cambodia was not due to natural disaster. It can be understood only in the context of a government without any viable economic base, which was kept fighting by becoming totally dependent on the United States for arms, money, and food. In the meantime, officials, officers, and businessmen exploited the war and the disruption of the economy in order to increase their own wealth, while the majority of the people could not buy enough food to sustain their families. Most important, however, is the fact that U.S. policy placed a concern for human suffering so far below a concern for avoiding the failure of its anti-Communist policy in Cambodia that it was prepared to accept mass starvation for an indefinite period in order to postpone the military defeat of its client.

The Economic Collapse of the GKR Zone

The problem of starvation in Phnom Penh and other cities during the war arose from the fact that the Lon Nol government steadily lost control of any economic base in the countryside until it came to rely entirely on the United States for its food supply. By the end of 1973, after the rice-surplus areas of Kompong Thom and Takeo had fallen, one after another, to the National United Front of Kampuchea (NUFK), the GKR was left with only partial control over the main rice-producing province of Battambang.[1]

From 2.46 million hectares in 1969, the total cultivated paddy land fell to only about 500,000 hectares in 1974.[2] At the same time even those rice-growing areas still under Phnom Penh's control showed a drop in yields. When the war began the average rice yield in Cambodia was about one metric ton per hectare—one of the lowest in Asia.[3] By 1974 yields had dropped even further due to the destruction of farm machinery, impressment of young men into the Lon Nol army, damage to croplands, shortages of seed and fertilizer, and the unfavorable ratio between the official purchase price of rice and the cost of fertilizer and pesticides.[4] Primarily because of loss of control over productive land, then, and secondarily because of lower yields in the remaining areas, paddy production in the Khmer Republic zone fell from a high of 3.8 million tons in 1969-70 to 493,000 tons (at a highly favorable estimate) in 1974-75—an 87 percent decline.[5] Thus Cambodia, which had exported some 230,000 tons of rice in 1968[6] had to import 282,000 tons during calendar year 1974 under the PL-480 program.[7]

At the same time, more than 2 million people were making their way to Phnom Penh and other cities; most of them were never registered with the government as refugees.[8] The population of Phnom Penh increased from a prewar total of about 600,000 to nearly 3 million.[9] Meanwhile, industrial production fell to only 42 percent of its prewar level, and total exports declined to insignificant amounts.[10]

As the productive base of the country was taken over by the revolutionary NUFK, and as the few remaining enclaves filled up with refugees, the Cambodian riel rapidly lost its value despite increased U.S. assistance. The GKR budget deficit increased as military spending soared from 24 billion riels in 1972 to 33 billion in 1973 and then to an estimated 69 billion in 1974 (which was 50 percent greater than the total liquid assets in the hands of the public at the end of December 1973).[11]

The drastic fall in rice production in the GKR zone and the increased isolation of Phnom Penh and other towns meant that the free market could no longer function effectively to distribute food. Market prices for food rose at a staggering rate: rice increased from 10 riels per kilogram in December 1971 to 125 riels per kilogram in December 1973.[12] The GKR policy of distributing rice to precinct, or *ilot*, officials for sale at an officially controlled price did not work. Since the government bought and sold rice at artificially low prices, much of Cambodia's own production, as well as large quantities of U.S.-imported rice, was smuggled into Vietnam or Thailand.[13] In addition, huge quantities were hoarded in anticipation of further price increases.[14]

Furthermore, the amount of rice imported by the United States was far less than was required to keep consumption in Phnom Penh at anywhere near normal levels. By late 1974 these imports provided enough for a daily distribution that varied between 500 and 700 metric tons.[15] The Agency for International Development (AID) director in Phnom Penh, Norman Sweet, stated in an interview in March 1975 that the amount needed to provide adequate nutrition for the population of Phnom Penh was about 1,000 tons per day.[16] Since the United States and the GKR were presumably basing their estimates on the commonly accepted figure of 2 million people in Phnom Penh,[17] rather than the nearly 3 million now believed to have lived in and around the city, it appears that the rice supply was only about one-third of what was needed to insure a minimum diet, assuming adequate distribution.

The final blow to the free market system was the NUFK's isola-

tion of Phnom Penh from the food-growing areas in the GKR
zone and from the deep-water port of Sihanoukville (known as
Kompong Som under the GKR). As small fly-by-night airlines
sprang into existence to transport food from the provinces into
Phnom Penh, wholesalers with transport contracts reportedly
made as much as 800 percent profit on each planeload of rice,
vegetables, meat, or fish brought to the capital, and the prices on
the free market reflected these profits.[18] In September 1974, in an
effort to stem the hoarding and smuggling, the official price of
rice was tripled to 137 riels per kilogram, but the following month
the free market price shot up again to 300 riels per kilogram.[19]
Moreover, the hoarding-profiteering cycle was not confined to
foodstuffs. Many medicines disappeared from the pharmacies,
only to reappear four months later, after the start of the January
1975 offensive, at eleven times the September price.[20]

In May 1974 it was estimated by the World Health Organization
that the average household head was making just enough to purchase the minimal requirements of rice.[21] After September 1974
even this was beyond the means of most families. An International
Monetary Fund study showed that a minimum diet for a six-
member household of two adults and four children cost 28,700
riels per month in September 1974 and increased to 35,100 riels
by November.[22] Few families could afford this, for the average
monthly income in the private sector was only about 33,000 riels
per month. Civil servants and military men made far less: basic
pay for the ordinary soldier was 15,802 riels per month, while
that of the highest commissioned officer was 22,000 riels per
month.[23] Since the military pay system was irregular at best and
usually subject to the thievery of corrupt officers, the families
of soldiers in the GKR army, the Force Armée Nationale Khmere
(or FANK), were one of the hardest hit groups in the population
under GKR control. Some workers, moreover, made only one-
sixth the amount believed required to feed the average-sized
household.[24] Even the small middle class was virtually wiped
out by the triple diget inflation (280 percent in 1974): Phnom
Penh's teachers, for example, earning one-third what they needed

to support their families, cut their teaching loads by two-thirds to protest soaring living costs.[25]

The price of rice continued to climb after the beginning of the NUFK offensive in January 1975, when the Mekong was successfully blocked, isolating Phnom Penh from all but air traffic. As the total amount of rice distributed daily in Phnom Penh was reduced from 600 to 545 metric tons,[26] the free market price rose from 300 to 340 riels per kilo by mid-February 1975.

Yet the official price was beyond the means of most people, and even if they had the money, there was simply not enough rice available on the official market to provide an adequate diet. In February 1975, the maximum a single family could obtain at the subsidized price was 2.75 kilos for each member every ten days, or 270 grams a day per person—only 60 percent of the 450 grams considered by the World Health Organization to be the absolute minimum nutritional requirement.[27]

This was the ration that was *supposed* to be made available through the official distribution system in the *ilots*. In fact, however, families could not even obtain that, in large part because of the diversion of rice by GKR officials into the black market and the hoarding of supplies on a massive scale. Many hundred-pound bags of rice simply disappeared from GKR warehouses, sold to the city's merchants.[28] According to an investigation by the GKR "controller general," by the middle of February thievery by local officials had reached the point that in one neighborhood in Phnom Penh, fully 46.3 percent of the rice that was supposed to be distributed had simply disappeared.[29] In March, several officials in western Phnom Penh reported that the amount available per person at the offical price in their *ilot* had fallen to 1.6 kilos every ten days, or less than 160 grams per day, because of such illegal diversions—a loss of 37 percent of the officially distributed rice.[30] Thus even if a family was fortunate enough to have the money to buy an entire ten-day allocation at the official price, it could only obtain 35 percent of the minimum daily nutritional requirement.

Equally important in considering the desperate situation in

Phnom Penh is the fact that few families could afford to buy meat, fish, or fruit. Until the economic collapse, Cambodians ate more fish and meat than the Vietnamese and Laotians, and this provided, along with abundant fruit, the protein and vitamins necessary to supplement rice in the Khmer diet.[31] As early as October 1971, however, meat, poultry, and fish had largely disappeared from the diet of the poor in Phnom Penh.[32] And by the beginning of 1975 the poor had virtually nothing to supplement what little rice they could purchase. As one voluntary relief worker said in February, Cambodian families "cannot even afford one banana for a child."[33]

Approximately 450,000 *registered* refugees in Phnom Penh were given a meager 150 grams of rice per day per person free from voluntary agencies. They also received some medical attention from clinics in the camps and some of the more seriously malnourished received high-protein nutritional supplements.[34] But for the hundreds of thousands of refugees who were not registered, and who had no employment or were underemployed, there was no assistance at all from either the United States or the GKR. Consequently, they, along with the wives and children of soldiers, were the ones who suffered the most from hunger and starvation.

The Growth of Starvation in Phnom Penh

United States and GKR authorities had plenty of warning about starvation in Phnom Penh. Seldom has a people's slide into severe malnourishment been so carefully recorded as it was in Cambodia, where both United States and international agencies observed and reported on it regularly. As early as October 1971, investigators from the U.S. General Accounting Office found that "lack of sufficient food" was "rapidly . . . becoming a serious problem." All but two of the many refugees they interviewed "stated that it was very difficult to obtain sufficient food for their families."[35] In September 1971 the representative of the International Red Cross estimated that it cost about $1.80 per day to adequately feed one person in the Phnom Penh area. But the daily earnings of the refugee families surveyed ranged from $.36 to $3, which had to feed between four and eleven people.[36]

In November 1973 a survey of nine refugee camps in and around Phnom Penh found that the 31 percent of the children under six in the worst camp, and the 16 percent under six in the best camp, were "severely malnourished."[37] In early 1974 the World Health Organization reported that half the children in Phnom Penh were believed to be moderately malnourished.[38] In mid-1974 a study mission sent to Indochina by the Senate Sub-committee on Refugees found the deterioration of the health of the population of Phnom Penh and other cities due to malnutrition already far advanced. Dr. David French of Boston University Medical School, a member of the mission, testified that "large numbers of children in Phnom Penh are currently suffering severe nutritional damage." He reported that medical personnel involved in relief work were convinced that malnutrition had already had serious effects on the children's growth and development and had destroyed their resistance to disease.[39]

After September 1974 the nutritional deterioration accelerated. It was analyzed in detail by the Office of the U.S. Department of State Inspector-General of Foreign Assistance, in a study carried out in Cambodia in February 1975. A comparison between weight-for-age and arm circumference-for-age data in August-September 1974 and January 1975 revealed a disastrous decline in nutritional status in only four months. The average body weight of two-year-old children sampled in September 1974 was 8.74 kilograms—already 17 percent less than the prewar average of 55 kilograms—indicating serious malnutrition. In January the average weight of the two-year-olds surveyed was 7.85 kilograms, 27 percent less than before the war.[40] Such a weight loss indicated a caloric intake during a year or longer of less than 60 percent of the minimum required to maintain body weight.[41]

These statistics, according to the Inspector-General's report, "confirmed the universal medical impression given us by those involved in Cambodia health and nutrition that children are starving

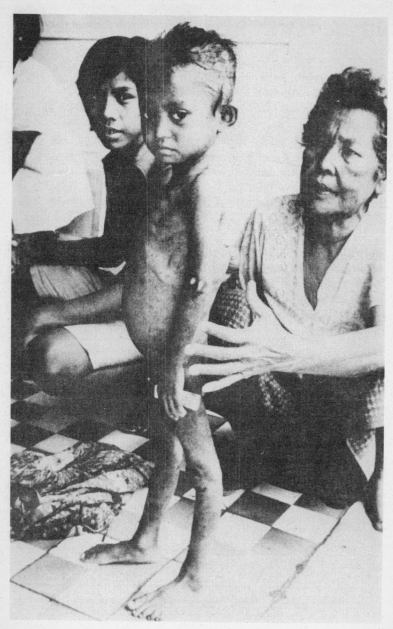

Starvation: Phnom Penh, January 1975.

to death."[42] The report noted that the number of children in "advanced stages" of kwashiorkor (extreme protein deficiency) and marasmus (severe caloric deficiency) had "increased dramatically over the last several months."[43] Kwashiorkor is easily recognized by swelling limbs and peeling skin, loss of appetite, and complete apathy. Fatty deposits infiltrate the heart, liver, kidneys, and brain, with certain death the result if the condition is not reversed. Marasmus, on the other hand, is marked by emaciation of the limbs and bloated stomach.[44] Many of the children of Phnom Penh and other cities suffered from both conditions at the same time.[45]

Starvation also worsened serious illness and caused death from normally minor diseases such as enteritis, flu, measles, and respiratory infections because of the children's loss of resistance.[46] In Neak Luong, where 25,000 civilians were receiving little food, Sydney Schanberg of the *New York Times* described this scene at a small Catholic Relief Services hospital:

> The children gathered by the dozens around a Western newsman. . . . Some have swollen bellies. Some are shrunken. A 10-year-old girl has dehydrated to the size of a 4-year-old. Harsh bronchial coughs come from their throats, marking the beginnings of pneumonia and tuberculosis. All have dysentery. Their noses run continuously. Their skins have turned scaly. Every scratch on their legs and arms becomes an ulcer.[47]

In addition, lack of hygiene, an unsafe water supply, and overcrowded conditions led to frequent epidemics of common diseases in Phnom Penh. There was a serious outbreak of measles in early 1975, for example, which was reported to have caused "especially high mortality in the 0-5-year age group, due to the poor nutritional state." Even more ominous were incidents of cholera reported in "clinically significant numbers" in Phnom Penh and in Neak Luong, where twenty deaths were reported. Vitamin A deficiency, which can lead to blindness, and beri-beri or Vitamin B^1 deficiency, also became increasingly prevalent as a result of eating polished U.S. rice rather than Cambodia's own less polished rice, and the absence of fruit and fish in the diet.[48]

Kwashiorkor, which is seldom found except among severely

malnourished children between the ages of two to four, was increasingly found among children as old as ten. By early February, according to Dr. Penelope Key of the World Vision Organization, it was common to see older children as severely malnourished as little ones. Adults, too, were suffering from starvation: all but two of the 130 mothers and grandmothers who brought children to the Tuol Kauk nutrition center were "moderately or severely anemic" due to malnourishment.[49]

A further illustration of the severity of the crisis was the extremely high rate of death among the severely malnourished children treated in Phnom Penh's clinics; many were simply too weak to be saved. At the Tuol Kauk nutrition center, between June and September 1974, 12 percent of the 345 children who entered with kwashiorkor or marasmus died.[50] The proportion of deaths to admissions continued to rise as the situation became more desperate. In December there were 26 deaths at the center, or 20 percent of admissions; in January the number increased to 49, or 36 percent of admissions.[51] At the Catholic Relief Services children's clinic, of the 10 to 15 children admitted daily an average of 3 died.[52] At the Red Cross children's clinic, which admitted 145 children with advanced cases of starvation during the last week in February alone, 65 children, or 46 percent of the total, died despite emergency treatment. Three weeks later the rate of death was even higher.[53]

These deaths were but the smallest tip of the iceberg. The nutrition centers treated only a low percentage of the children brought to their doors. The World Vision child nutrition center, for example, had to turn away 1,758 severely malnourished children during the two-month period from December 1974 to February 1975 because of lack of beds, accepting only 235 worst cases.[54] Thus only 13 percent of those who actually went to that center received help. The Office of the Inspector-General, departing from its normally clinical tone, commented: "It requires little imagination to picture these wretchedly frail and sickly little bodies, borne away in their weak mothers' arms, carried to an alley somewhere, to die; certain to suffer, untreated, unhospitalized, unfed."[55]

Most of the starving and gravely ill children were probably

never even brought to the clinics because their parents had given up hope for their survival. A Red Cross doctor noticed a common pattern of behavior among the poor in the final months of the war; when a family had several starving children, the parents would "decide unconsciously not to give any more to the weakest child."[56]

Although no effort was made to estimate how many people were dying each day from starvation, it is clear that the numbers were very high. Dr. Gay Alexander, medical director for Catholic Relief Services from March 1974 to March 1975, declared in March 1975 that "hundreds are dying of malnutrition every day."[57] Voluntary agency personnel, refugees, and residents of Phnom Penh all agreed by early March that the number of deaths from starvation was "increasing daily."[58] Furthermore, according to Dr. Alexander the children of Cambodia were "on the brink" and could "slip down very easily."[59] Red Cross doctors were quoted as saying that "thousands and thousands" of children "may be tipping over."[60] An eyewitness in Phnom Penh in March described seeing "thousands of small children, their bellies swollen from hunger," who "waited for slow death from kwashiorkor and marasmus."[61]

Based on these accounts, if a conservative estimate of 250 deaths per day from starvation is used the total for March alone comes to nearly 8,000 people. And the total number for the last five months of the war must have been at least 15,000 and possibly far more.

Furthermore, those children who did not die from starvation will suffer permanent damage to their bodies and minds due to the severe malnutrition. As Dr. Key observed in March, "This generation is going to be a lost generation of children. Malnutrition is going to affect their numbers and their mental capacities. So, as well as knocking off a generation of young men, the war is knocking off a generation of children."[62]

The Human Cost of Corruption

While the masses of refugees and urban poor were starving, other Cambodians were living in unprecedented luxury. Cambodian society under the GKR was afflicted with a military and civilian elite which had acquired a taste for upper-class European lifestyles that, with U.S. aid, could be indulged as never before. Corruption had existed under Prince Sihanouk, and was publicly discussed as a problem, but it had been limited in its scope and ostentation.[63] With his overthrow, however, the officers and civil servants whose ambition to become a new economic elite had been thwarted suddenly had virtually unlimited opportunities to exploit their positions for profit. A whole new caste of military officers emerged as a formerly ceremonial army burgeoned into a military bureaucracy. With the wartime disintegration of the Cambodian economy, the vast increase in U.S. aid, and the absence of any effective control over their behavior, the military and civilian elite became the beneficiary of an unprecedented explosion of wealth.

The primary source of this wealth, of course, was the ammunition, weapons and other military supplies, medicines, and rice that they sold to merchants, who in time resold them on the free market or to Cambodian and Vietnamese revolutionary forces. The chief of the U.S. Military Equipment Distribution Team (MEDT) estimated in February 1973 that the FANK was padding its troop strength by 10 to 15 percent. The GAO in turn estimated that between $750,000 and $1 million went into the pockets of corrupt commanders *every month* from paychecks for "phantom" or nonexistent soldiers.[64] (The *New York Times* had earlier estimated the rake-off from "phantom soldiers" to be even higher—$2 million a month.)[65] High military officials also made large fortunes on the diversion to the free market of military supplies, particularly fuel, that were provided for the FANK under U.S. military aid programs.[66] By some estimates, fully half of the $350 million in U.S. military aid provided in 1974 was never used for military purposes but was sold by the generals, colonels, and majors for private profit.[67]

As the military and political crisis of the Phnom Penh regime dragged on, high-ranking officers became increasingly involved in schemes for profiting from the war. Late in 1973 the commander at Takeo and the governors of Koh Kong and Kampot provinces were relieved of their duties for having illegally exported more than three thousand tons of U.S.-made brass shellcastings worth about $3 million through private businessmen.[68] The trafficking in goods became so important to the governmental elite that there was an unspoken understanding that individuals in the most lucrative posts would be rotated every few months. Thus Phnom Penh observers spoke of the "merry-go-round" of executive positions. It was even charged that new provinces were created in order to let more officers in on the profits.[69]

And so, while the populations of Phnom Penh and other towns were plunged into hunger and starvation, the living standards of the elite rose spectacularly. Lower- and middle-ranking military and civilian officials were able to make large fortunes, and a whole new suburb of Phnom Penh was spawned for the magnificent villas of this new class of wealthy officers and civil servants. An officer who was eased out of his position in 1973, Major Yin Kheng of the Third Military District, fled to France with an estimated 200 million riels (about $800,000), while another 50 million riels were transferred to his ten-year-old son. His furnished mansion, a multistoreyed apartment house, a house on stilts, and some warehouses were confiscated by the government.[70] But Major Yin Kheng was only a small-fry as far as Phnom Penh-style corruption was concerned: General Lon Non, the president's brother, and the generals allied with him were reported to be making millions of dollars a year. Lon Non left the country in 1973 with an estimated $90 million made primarily by selling arms and ammunition, and by extortion.[71] As for Lon Nol himself, Kong Horth, a former lieutenant junior grade assigned to the naval accounting office, has charged that the president ordered $1 million a year diverted from the U.S. naval aid program for his personal use.[72]

Even in the darkest days of starvation in Phnom Penh, the expensive lifestyle of the elite was not visibly affected. While the government's "austerity" program kept the poor neighborhoods in darkness because of power cutoffs, the air-conditioned homes of the wealthy continued to receive full power and the lights went on at the Cercle Sportif for evening tennis players.[73] "For the few privileged elite," an American correspondent wrote in April 1975, "the good life of tennis, nightclubs, expensive French meals and opulent brandy-drenched dinner parties went on almost to the very end, while the vast majority of the city's swollen population sank into deeper and deeper misery."[74]

Given the corruption and lack of social conscience of Phnom Penh's governing elite, it is hardly surprising that the Lon Nol regime did nothing to prevent massive deaths from starvation: as a popular Phnom Penh student slogan ran, "Corruption + incompetence = the people's hunger."[75] From the start, the GKR manifested little or no concern about the human suffering. Rather than attempting to register all those who had lost their homes and could not support their families, the Lon Nol regime discouraged people from expecting any help from the government. There was no overall program to deal with the problem of war victims and no specific program to provide even temporary relief for refugees.[76] One voluntary agency official with experience in working with the GKR observed in 1973, "You are not working from a base where you have a functioning sense of social service within the Cambodian government."[77]

Indeed, a "sense of social service" was so alien to the Cambodian governmental elite that the few foreign-sponsored efforts to provide relief simply put more money in the pockets of wealthy officials. When the government of Italy donated $10,000 for refugee assistance, only half of it even made it to the Director-General of Refugees, the other half having been taken by Lon Non, supposedly for "aiding Cambodians residing in South Vietnam."[78] After visiting Cambodia in a study mission, Senator Edward Brooke, apparently reflecting official U.S. Mission views, commented that a "high probability exists that relief aid would become another temptation for extensive graft and corruption if channeled through the existing governmental structure."[79]

The corruption and incompetence of the GKR also resulted, as we have seen, in the disappearance of a large proportion of the rice that was supposed to be sold on the official market at controlled prices. Because of massive diversion and the unwillingness of the GKR to carry out even the simplest program of food relief, Cambodian children needlessly starved.

U.S. Policy and the Problem of Starvation

In the larger context of the Cambodian war, however, the GKR government elite cannot be held primarily responsible for the starvation in its own zone. More than any other government in the world, it existed only at the sufferance of the United States. An analysis of the total resources used by the GKR to remain in control of Phnom Penh and a few provincial enclaves shows that by 1974 domestic revenues accounted for only 2.2 percent of these resources, while 95.1 percent came from U.S. assistance.[80] (The remaining 2.7 percent came from other foreign assistance.)[81] Given this nearly total dependence on U.S. aid, it was really the United States which bore the responsibility for the continuation of the war, month after month, year after year.

Only the United States could make and enforce a decision that Cambodians would not starve to death. But the United States did not have sufficient concern for the problem of starvation to sacrifice interests that loomed larger in U.S. policy. The overriding U.S. aim was to avoid a humiliating defeat by forcing the NUFK to negotiate a settlement with the Lon Nol regime.

The U.S. aid program was devoted almost entirely to the support of the GKR military effort—either through the military assistance program, or indirectly, through the economic aid programs. The latter provided goods to be sold through the existing official commercial distribution system and thus generated Cambodian currency for the GKR military budget. During fiscal years 1971, 1972, and 1973, the United States provided $748 million in assistance to the GKR, only $1.1 million of which went for assistance to refugees. Virtually all the rest supported either military equipment or military salaries.[82]

In spite of the fact that hundreds of thousands of refugees fled their homes in the countryside because of U.S. bombing,[83] officials took the position from the beginning of the war that the United States had no responsibility for taking care of those war victims. In October 1971, the General Accounting Office (GAO) reported:

> According to the U.S. Ambassador to Cambodia, it has been the policy of the United States not to become involved with the problem of civilian war victims in Cambodia. . . . He said that, since the United States was providing military and economic aid to Cambodia, it was the policy of the United States to encourage other countries—which could not provide military assistance because of their own internal political situations—to assist Cambodia with humanitarian needs.[84]

Apparently the U.S. embassy had made it clear to the Cambodian government that it did not wish to be asked for humanitarian assistance. The U.S. ambassador informed the GAO that it was "not likely that the Cambodian government will request humanitarian assistance from the United States even if the civilian war victim problem becomes much more severe than it has been." This was because, according to the GAO, "Cambodian government officials realize that the United States is a source for necessary military assistance and desire that any assistance obtained from the United States be channeled toward the advancement of the war effort."[85] In other words, the United States did not wish to divert any of its aid from the military effort to food, housing, or medical care for refugees.

The official explanation for the continued refusal of the U.S. government to launch a major program of food and medical care for war victims was the GKR's "lack of administrative experience in refugee relief" (a euphemism for corruption and lack of interest in social welfare), as well as the ceiling of two hundred authorized personnel imposed by Congress on the U.S. Mission, which, it was said, "precluded using additional direct-hire personnel" for refugee relief.[86]

U.S. officials justified their lack of concern with the plight of

Phnom Penh's refugees: Cambodiana Hotel, March 1975.

refugees by arguing that relatives and friends would take care of them, so that "sizeable population movements" could take place "without distress and without much government involvement."[87] Even after two years of war, and after Red Cross doctors began reporting serious malnutrition in Phnom Penh, the State Department continued to claim that the "expanded family system" could absorb "most" of the refugees.[88] This was, of course, a thin rationalization, since reliance on friends or relatives was the only choice open as long as the GKR had no program of its own. The State Department also tried to minimize the problem by grossly misrepresenting the size of Phnom Penh's swollen wartime population. The commonly accepted estimate of the population in January 1971 was 1.5 million people, but State Department spokesmen claimed in public testimony to Congress that it was only 400,000.[89]

In late 1972, long after it had become impossible to deny the desperate situation of the refugees in Cambodia, the U.S. Mission essentially dumped the problem in the lap of the voluntary agencies by offering grants in the next year of $2.5 million to three private American agencies and one international agency for refugee assistance.[90] In November 1973 the Mission added a "senior refugee resettlement adviser," a "medical administrator," and a "voluntary agency coordinator" to the single refugee adviser position created in late 1972 to deal with the entire problem of war victims in Cambodia.[91]

The voluntary agencies could do little to help the refugees without food. And the PL-480 program, which the American public thinks of as a program of free food for the poor and starving, was actually used to generate Cambodian riels for the military budget rather than to feed the hungry. The program has two separate aspects worldwide: title II, under which the United States donates food for free distribution to the needy, and title I, under which it gives food or lends it on concessionary terms to a government for sale through commercial or official channels to generate local currencies for military spending. In Cambodia, title II was scarcely used at all. Altogether, in fiscal years 1973 and 1974 the United States spent less than $50,000 for free food distribution through voluntary agencies, even as hundreds of thousands of Cambodians slid into chronic malnutrition.[92] During the first half of fiscal year 1975, beginning in July 1974, the Agency for International Development (AID) spent a total of $72.5 million under PL-480 for food shipments to Cambodia, but only $1 million of that was used to support free distribution.[93]

The indifference of U.S. officials to the suffering of the Cambodian poor drew a strong protest from Senator Harrison Williams of New Jersey, who pointed out in April 1975 that, in congressional testimony taken in 1974, "warnings were given that large numbers of Cambodian children were beginning to experience malnutrition and that a crisis was emerging." Even so, he said, "little was done to meet the crisis by either the U.S. government or the Cambodian government." In spite of the extraordinary airlift into Phnom Penh, Williams said, the administration had "disregarded the need to move food into the city until forced to begin a program in order to induce Congress to pass the $222 million supplemental military aid request."[94]

In March 1975 AID announced that it was providing just over $15 million to voluntary agencies to buy rice from title I stocks for distribution to registered refugees. But that furnished only 50 tons of rice for free distribution to officially recorded refugees, barely touching the surface of the massive hunger that was engulfing Phnom Penh.[95] As Deputy AID Administrator John E. Murphy admitted at the time, "Ironically, it is the population, the regular population of Phnom Penh that is suffering, because they are not on the list of registered refugees and are not eligible for AID and must buy whatever they eat . . . and the money to buy the rice that is there is just not in the people's hands."[96]

Some months later the State Department, in response to an inquiry by Congressman Robert Edgar of Pennsylvania, explained its "inability to respond to the malnutrition problem" by citing the difficulty of recruiting sufficient personnel for voluntary agencies to distribute rice.[97] It did not mention the fact that the U.S. Mission itself was unwilling to spare more than a handful of people from the task of running the war. Nor did it bother to explain why it was financing a government so corrupt that it was unable to organize any food distribution program itself.

The State Department also cited "physical limitations on the amount of rice and medicines that could be airlifted into Phnom Penh under fire at the city's airport," arguing that it was "physically impossible to supply the required amount of foodstuffs by air each day."[98] Again, the official explanation neglected to mention that the United States was at the same time bringing in 565 tons of ammunition each day.[99] Airlifting food instead of war materiel would thus have *doubled* the amount of food available to the population of Phnom Penh. One AID official, trying to explain the disparity between officially estimated needs and the planned U.S. airlift, suggested lamely that "over a period of time" the population "could get along on something less than normal."[100]

Many of the voluntary agency personnel who confronted starvation on a daily, face-to-face basis recognized that Cambodian children were dying because of the refusal of the United States to put human needs ahead of its support for the regime. Robert Beck of World Vision said, "Kids are dying who shouldn't die. They die in our arms. It's hard to believe. There's no excuse for it."[101] Dr. Beat Richner, a Red Cross volunteer who worked at the pediatric hospital in Phnom Penh, told a reporter, "The only way to stop this catastrophe is to stop the war."[102] And Dr. Gay Alexander of Catholic Relief Services called for an immediate end to military aid to the GKR "to end this senseless war."[103]

But instead of moving to end the suffering, the Ford administration used all of its influence to keep the war going, hoping that the spring rains would widen the Mekong and make it possible to break the National United Front's control of the supply route and give the Lon Nol regime one more year of life. As Lt.-General H. M. Fish, director of the Pentagon's Defense Security Assistance Agency, testified before Congress on February 3, 1975, "We seek only to keep them alive and fighting through the remainder of this fiscal year."[104] The temporary survival of an anti-Communist regime in Cambodia was Washington's primary concern, and if tens of thousands of Cambodian children had to starve to keep Phnom Penh in the war for still another dry season, that was apparently an acceptable human cost.

2
The Evacuation
of Phnom Penh

The Evacution and the Media

When the NUFK moved the people from Phnom Penh and other cities to the countryside in April 1975, the leading print and electronic media organizations in the United States lost no time in epressing their indignation. "One can only imagine the suffering and degradation," intoned the *Wall Street Journal*. "Clearly the new rulers of Cambodia have invented a new brand of cruelty."[1] The *Washington Star* labeled the evacuation "a monstrosity of epic proportions,"[2] while columnist Jack Anderson pronounced it "the greatest atrocity since the Nazis herded Jews into the gas chambers."[3]

Some commentators saw it as an attempt by the revolutionaries to punish or "purify" the city-dwellers, because of the ideology they were presumed to represent.[4] Others asserted that the Cambodian authorities were trying to transform Cambodia into a primitive agrarian communal state, eliminating the "modern" influence of the cities.[5] Most commentators appeared to share *Newsweek*'s judgment: "Clearly, any government that would send millions of city-dwellers to an uncertain fate in the ravaged countryside did not place much value on individual human lives."[6]

This attack on the new Cambodian government coincided with the official position of the Ford administration, which was interested in making the victors a target of public and congressional hostility in the wake of the U.S. defeat in Indochina. Secretary of State Kissinger called the evacuation "an atrocity of major proportions," while Assistant Secretary of State Philip Habib testified that it went "beyond the bounds of moral decency."[7]

One might have expected this kind of chorus of condemnation to have followed the discovery of volumes of compelling first-person testimony, but in fact its basis was an account written three weeks after the evacuation by a single journalist, Sydney Schanberg of the *New York Times*,[8] which has since earned him the Pulitzer prize for foreign reporting. The article was a weak foundation for the massive historical judgment rendered by the news media. It contained no details or eyewitness reports on how the evacuation was carried out in terms of food, medical treatment, transportation, or the general treatment of the evacuees. Nor was there any extensive analysis of the reasons Schanberg attributed to the revolutionary leadership for the action. But the article did quote extensively from Western observers who were in the French embassy with Schanberg, and who denounced the evacuation as "genocide" and the Cambodian revolutionaries as "crazy."

The tone of the article—and the banner headline it received in the *Times*—were set by Schanberg's lead sentence: "The victorious Cambodian Communists, who marched into Phnom Penh on April 17 and ended five years of war in Cambodia, are carrying out a peasant revolution that has thrown the entire country into upheaval." The implications of the article were twofold: first, that the point of the agrarian revolution in Cambodia was to force everyone from the cities to become peasants—rather than to reorganize rural society in order to increase the country's productive potential; and second, that the "upheaval" created by the evacuation disrupted what would otherwise have been an orderly and painless transition from war to peace. Schanberg raised the question of whether the move was "just cold brutality, a cruel and sadistic law of the jungle," or whether it was seen by the Khmer revolutionaries as necessary in order to "build a new society literally starting from the beginning." In such an "unbending view," Schanberg declared, "people who represent the old ways and those considered weak or unfit would be expendable and would be weeded out." Perhaps, he suggested, the evacuation might have been both "cruel" and "ideological."

With his preconceived notion about a cruel and fanatical Cambodian leadership ready to carry out a genocidal purge of society to rid it of the "weak and unfit," Schanberg found it unnecessary to examine alternative explanations for the evacuation, and the reader finds no hint that conditions in Phnom Penh and the country as a whole might offer one.

The rest of the news media quickly adopted Schanberg's point of view, as well as the substance of his article.[9] The way in which the "cruel" and "doctrinaire" character of the evacuation was turned into hard fact is a classic case of an instinctive political response by an institution that interprets events in conformity with the dominant ideological views of society. The news media did not feel it necessary to have any specific facts, or to examine the entire social and economic contest of postwar Cambodia, in order to pass harsh judgment on the revolutionary government. They condemned the evacuation a priori, because commentators and editorialists *expected* revolutionaries to be "unbending" and to have no regard for human life, and because they were totally unprepared to examine the possibility that radical change might be required in that particular situation.

Had the media approached the story of postwar Cambodia as a problem to be investigated by assessing all the available information, they would have found it difficult to avoid the conclusion that the evacuation was the result not of doctrinaire principles unrelated to reality, but that it was prompted by a concern for the most basic and urgent needs of the population. Moreover, they would have found that food, water, rent, and medical care were provided along the way—contrary to the "death march" image fostered in the minds of most Americans.

Phnom Penh: The Need for Radical Action

The evacuation of the cities of Cambodia cannot be understood without underscoring the fact that relatively few of the nearly 3 million people allegedly "uprooted" and dispatched on a "forced march" into the countryside were true city-dwellers at all. In 1970, when the war began, Phnom Penh was a city of about 600,000; 100,000 to 150,000 of these were Vietnamese, who fled or were deported after the Lon Nol regime carried out a series of massacres against the Vietnamese community in April 1970.[10] So five of every six Cambodians who lived in the capital in April 1975 were in fact peasant refugees who had fled to the city. The more than 2 million refugees in the Phnom Penh area did not have to be "forced" to return to the countryside, since they had no reason to remain in Phnom Penh once the war had stopped. The significance of this cannot be overstated, because it means that even before the war ended, the NUFK had to have a comprehensive plan for resettling this massive refugee population on agricultural land. And it had to manage this return in such a way as to minimize the disruption of the economy and to maximize the use of their labor for urgent agricultural tasks.

This resettlement was to be a monumental reorganizational task, involving between one-third and one-half of the entire population of the country. It could not be limited, moreover, to providing food for those returning to the countryside in order to tide them over until the next harvest. The countryside was greatly changed. Whole villages had been wiped out, great stretches of rice fields damaged or abandoned. More than 90 percent of the houses in the most heavily bombed parts of the country had been destroyed.[11] Further, the war had profoundly altered the pattern of rural settlement and cultivation, and returning refugees would have to be integrated into existing production cooperatives, often on land some distance from their original homes, or grouped together in new settlements. And this vast reverse immigration could not wait, for every day of delay would have a human cost in death and suffering.

Above all else, the NUFK leadership had to be concerned with food and health. The concentration of a large part of the popula-

Peasants fleeing the war for the city, 1973.

tion in the cities, where they were unproductive and totally dependent on foreign aid, posed grave dangers. On the one hand, any
attempt to maintain an adequate supply of rice for the urban
population would have disrupted the existing and highly organized
system of agricultural production; on the other hand, the extremely overcrowded conditions, combined with the breakdown of all
normal public services, made the outbreak of a major epidemic
highly probable.

When the war ended there was only enough food in Phnom
Penh to last a few days.[12] Pleading for international assistance
was no answer; it would take weeks, perhaps even months, before
international agencies could mobilize their resources. Nor was
there any question of putting the fate of masses of hungry people
in the cities in the hands of the U.S. government, whose policies
had been responsible for the war and the mass starvation that had
already killed so many. In addition, the United States was apparently *counting* on food shortages in the cities to make it possible for right-wing elements to seize power again: according to
Deputy Premier Ieng Sary, a document detailing a plan to overthrow the government within six months was discovered by
revolutionary forces in Phnom Penh. The plan was based on the
assumption that the NUFK would not be able to feed the popula-

tion of the city, and that the situation would be ripe for violent disorders within a few months.[13]

The Cambodian leaders did not need to depend on foreign relief to feed the urban population, however. Food had been stocked in the countryside in advance in order to take care of returnees. Further, secondary crops were there, with which to supplement the evacuees' diet. Some vegetables, such as green beans, could be grown in only eighty days.[14] As Ieng Sary later pointed out, "By going to the countryside, our peasants have potatoes, bananas, and all kinds of food."

Moreover, it made little sense to try to move the food to an unproductive urban population. Ieng Sary explained, "We did not have sufficient transportation to move food into the capital."[15] The People's National Liberation Armed Forces of Kampuchea (PNLAFK), unlike either the Vietnamese or the Laotian revolutionary armies in 1975, were largely self-sufficient in supplies, with very little outside military assistance and no known economic aid.[16] During the war the only fuel available to the NUFK was captured or purchased from the FANK. Once the United States no longer provided it, the NUFK had to trade for fuel across the border in Thailand.[17] Thus a massive effort to truck food into Phnom Penh would have required a large part of this very limited supply, diverting fuel from other vital needs to support a swollen urban center that would have been able to produce nothing in exchange.

Even more important, the labor of the more than 3 million people in Phnom Penh and the other cities was desperately needed in order to help bring in the dry season harvest and to prepare the rice fields for the primary rainy season crop, which would be harvested in late 1975.[18] The need for agricultural labor was at a peak just as the war was ending. With only about half of the population already working in the fields, the additional efforts of the people from the cities would make the difference between a rice deficit or self-sufficiency in 1976. The 500,000 to 600,000 urban dwellers would, by growing their own food, by freeing others from the task of getting food to them, substantially increase the total produced. By remaining unproductive during the crucial months, on the other hand, they would reduce the amount of food available to everyone. For all these reasons, the NUFK leaders believed that "We had to solve the problem of food by ourselves on the basis of self-reliance."[19]

As the war came a close, the Cambodian leaders were also faced with the increasing threat of the outbreak of an epidemic, fostered by a combination of unsanitary conditions, overcrowding, and general malnutrition. Garbage collection deteriorated, then came to a halt. In the last weeks, mounds of trash could be seen burning in the streets.[20] Lack of pure water became a serious health hazard,[21] since, as the U.S. Inspector-General of Foreign Assistance reported in March, contaminated water supplies present "the potential for the spread of epidemics of cholera and typhoid fever."[22] (Cholera had in fact been reported in February.) The State Department report concluded: "Unsanitary living conditions in Phnom Penh caused by crowding and the influx of refugees into the city create a health hazard and present a danger of epidemics."[23]

As the collapse of the Lon Nol government approached, this danger grew. French doctors from the Calmette hospital told one Western journalist of reports of increased numbers of dead rats in the streets, and expressed fears of epidemics of cholera and typhoid.[24] In the days just prior to April 17, doctors began belatedly to inoculate some people on the streets against cholera, but it was a case of too little, too late.[25] A Khmer resident of Phnom Penh, describing the evacuation to a friend in the United States, wrote: "At the time that our families were evacuated from the city, cholera was spreading rapidly everywhere."[26] The NUFK's concern about epidemics in the city was reflected in the fact that the PNLAFK soldiers who organized the exodus administered cholera vaccine on the spot to the evacuees. As one Cambodian eyewitness recalled later, "The liberators distributed medicine, but it was insufficient, because the number of people was too large."[27] Evacuees from Phnom Penh, interviewed later in Thailand, have confirmed that vaccine was given out by the NUFK.[28]

By the time the NUFK took over Phnom Penh, moreover, the

city was almost completely without normal public services. There had been systematic sabotage of major public facilities, including the water filtration plant, the electric power plant, the national bank, and the docks, lighthouse, and other facilities at the port of Phnom Penh.[29] Thus the city lacked power, drinking water, and the ability to bring in goods by river.

The combined threats of starvation and epidemic were clearly on the minds of the Cambodian leaders when they planned the evacuation. According to the PNLAFK commander who negotiated the transfer of foreign nationals at the Thai border in early May, the decision was reached at a meeting in February. The commander told an American journalist that the evacuation was considered necessary to save the population of Phnom Penh from epidemic and starvation.[30] The same reasons were cited by Cambodian officials in discussions with Swedish Ambassador Kaj Bjoerk, the first Western diplomat to visit Phnom Penh after the war.[31]

The clearest evidence that the evacuation was prompted by concrete conditions is what was done with those cities afterward. In the first weeks after the evacuation, the cities, which were being referred to in the United States as "ghost towns" that had been left to return to jungle, were rehabilitated. Soldiers collected the accumulated rubbish, repaired public buildings and factories damaged by sabotage, and prepared for the return of the workers.[32] By mid-summer there were reports that housing had been restored and that residents were moving in.[33] At the same time, factories began production, beginning with textile and dry-cell battery factories.[34] By mid-August some seventy small and larger factories were back in operation.[35] Deputy Premier Ieng Sary said in September 1975 that there were approximately 100,000 people in Phnom Penh again, with further increases expected as productive facilities were restored and expanded.[36] Prince Sihanouk, in an interview with the Paris newspaper *Liberation*, noted that NUFK leaders intended to increase the population of the capital to 300,000 in the near future.[37] Bjoerk was told in March 1976 that there were between 100,000 and 200,000 people in the city.[38] Thus the cities have not only not been abandoned, but have been rehabilitated and given an appropriate role in the country's economic development.

Although it is clear that it was immediate human needs and longer term economic considerations that made the evacuation of the cities an urgent necessity, the move also helped the NUFK to quickly gain control over armed saboteurs and underground agents linked with the United States. There is considerable evidence that large numbers of these agents were planning to remain in Phnom Penh to carry out sabotage operations and to organize for a later attempt to overthrow the new government,[39] and the headquarters and leadership of the counter-revolutionary organization were in fact discovered and their apparatus destroyed.[40] Public facilities and a great deal of housing were damaged or razed.[41] There were many reports of grenades thrown by commandoes,[42] and foreign observers in the French embassy reported that "huge fires" were visible during the two weeks that followed the NUFK takeover, and that some neighborhoods were destroyed.[43] If underground agents had counted on the swollen population of Phnom Penh to provide them with easy cover for their operations, the evacuation dealt a fatal blow to the plan. They were either trapped in the city and could be tracked down, or were separated as the population was dispersed.

The "Death March" Charge

The evacuation of Phnom Penh has been repeatedly portrayed in the news media as a "death march" in which the population was forced into the countryside without providing it with food, water, or medical care, and in which the very young, the aged, the sick, and the wounded were forced to travel many miles on foot. The *New York Times* declared, in an editorial calling the move a "crime," that "one-third to one-half of the population was forced by the Communists at gunpoint to walk into the countryside in tropical temperatures and monsoon rains without organized provision of food, water, shelter, physical security or medical care."[44] This version of the evacuation was fostered by U.S government statements, including "intelligence documents," such as one leaked to Jack Anderson that quoted "doctors" among the refugees as saying that the authorities "provided no food, water or medicine throughout the long march."[45]

This charge is supported neither by the reports of numerous witnesses in Phnom Penh and the immediate vicinity, nor by interviews with Cambodian refugees conducted by journalists in Thailand. On the contrary, these accounts portray an evacuation that was planned in detail to ease the hardship of the move. An organization for processing and assisting the evacuees was set up, including one reception center some miles from Phnom Penh and another in the region where evacuees were to be resettled. At the first center, the evacuees were registered on mimeographed sheets on which they wrote their names, ages, occupations, family backgrounds, and other information. They were then directed toward a particular region, depending on where the family was originally from. At the second center they were met by a local committee, which assigned them land to cultivate.[46]

There is abundant first-hand evidence that the NUFK planned for the provision of necessities during the trip. A number of accounts, from both foreigners and Cambodian refugees, agree that rice was distributed to the evacuees along the route from stocks that had been collected in anticipation.[47] One American journalist reported seeing "relay stations and rest stops along the road out of Phnom Penh, where Khmer Rouge troops—mostly women— and Buddhist monks supplied refugees with food and water."[48] In addition, according to European observers who left the capital along with the first wave of evacuees, both rice and dried fish were sold along the way at one-third their price in Phnom Penh.[49] Father Jacques Engelmann, a Benedictine priest with nearly two decades of experience in Cambodia, wrote that, "There was enough food for everyone. At night, they would stop to cook the rice and sleep."[50] More than a dozen Cambodian refugees, interviewed in Thailand, said they had received enough food— primarily rice—on the trip.[51]

The image of evacuees being mistreated and driven to exhaustion is also contradicted by these accounts. None of the refugees interviewed in Thailand reported having been mistreated by the soldiers during the evacuation.[52] Father Engelmann reported that the priests who accompanied the evacuation "were not witness to any cruelties."[53] Jerome and Jocelyne Steinbach, who taught in Cambodia for two years prior to the liberation of Phnom Penh and who observed the beginning of the evacuation, recount how the soldiers went about getting people ready to leave:

On April 18, a group of soldiers passed before the door and said, "You must leave." If no one answered, someone would go by a second time repeating, "You must leave." Then a third time . . . and thus throughout the day, constantly, the same phrase. Until the day when the neighborhood had to be totally cleared: then, ready or not, one had to leave immediately. But even at the last moment, there was no brutality, no anger.[54]

These eyewitness accounts also indicate that the evacuees moved at a comfortable pace. A retired French military officer, married to a Khmer, reported that he saw the columns of evacuees move slowly and stop often for rest. Although the refugees wanted to stop longer than the soldiers charged with getting them to their destination would permit, the column moved only one or two kilometers between rests.[55] Two Swiss male nurses who saw the columns making their way south said that the people could move as rapidly or as slowly as they wished.[56] According to the refugees interviewed in Thailand, the trip from Phnom Penh to the first center took eight days to cover about twenty miles, or 2.5 miles a day.[57] Even at a very slow walking pace, that would have permitted three or four hours of rest for every mile walked.

Schanberg's report reached an emotional pitch in the statement that "No one has been excluded—even the very old, the very young, the sick and the wounded have been forced out onto the roads. . . ."[58] This charge is also belied by the account of those who witnessed the evacuation firsthand. While all these categories of people were moved out of the city along with everyone else, eyewitnesses describe an organized effort to transport the sick and aged in trucks and motor cars confiscated for that purpose.[59] A New Zealander who passed through several Cambodian villages with his Khmer wife reported that they slept in the same house as an elderly woman who had been transported by truck from Phnom Penh. "She told us that she refused to leave her house if she was forced to walk, so a cadre from the PNLAFK arranged for her to be transported by truck." The same woman told them that other elderly people had also been transported by truck.[60] The two Swiss nurses witnessed a similar scene in which four elderly people told the soldiers that they were too old to walk "even a kilometer." The soldiers immediately ordered a jeep to carry them.[61] There thus appears to be ample evidence that the "death march" characterization of the evacuation is unfounded.

The Hospitals of Phnom Penh

But what of the emptying of the hospitals by the Communist forces? Western observers have charged that, regardless of the reason for the exodus, it was inexcusable to force patients to abandon the hospitals and join the throngs on the road back to the countryside. Here again, hostility to the revolutionary Cambodian government has been allowed to prevail over regard for the facts. Examination of medical realities in Cambodia at the end of the war, and of actual NUFK policy, suggests that the purpose of this move was actually to save lives and give the best possible care to the sick and the wounded.

In the first place, a survey of medical conditions and the medical facilities that existed in Phnom Penh before the NUFK took over shows without doubt that the temporary clearing of most hospitals, far from being inhumane, was an act of mercy for the patients. It was recognized early in the war that the system of medical care in the GKR zone was totally inadequate. In 1973, for example, Preah Ket Melea hospital, one of the four government hospitals in Phnom Penh, was reported to have more than three times the number of patients it could adequately handle and lacked basic medicines and routine hospital materials—antibiotics, sterile dressings, syringes, and stethoscopes.[62] The modern equipment the hospital did have, including operating room lights and sterilization equipment, was rendered largely inoperable by continual power shortages.[63]

Another of the four major hospitals, the Soviet-Khmer Friendship Hospital, was considered by U.S. officials to be "extremely crowded, poorly equipped, unsanitary, and understaffed" as early as October 1971.[64] For a total of 1009 patients, it had only 512 beds and 27 doctors, instead of the 80 needed to provide minimum care.[65] Four years later the situation had deteriorated even further, with 300 more patients and only 1 additional doctor. Conditions in the hospital were graphically described by one eyewitness in March 1975 as follows:

> In the Khmer-Sovietique hospital, more than 1,300 patients struggled for survival last week. Doctors, nurses, medical corpsmen, drugs, and plasma were scarce; malaria, tuberculosis, and dysentery were rampant. Out of desperation, overworked staffers in some wards tied wounded men to their beds to prevent them from breaking open their wounds and sutures. Flies covered the face of one such patient, who could only shake his head feebly in a vain attempt to keep them from crawling into his mouth.[66]

Medical care had always received a low priority in both GKR and U.S. policy, as was reflected in the GKR's budgetary allocations for health. The World Health Organization recommends that to provide adequate health care, 10 percent of the national budget of a developing country *not* at war be allocated to the Ministry of Health.[67] A nation involved in a highly destructive war should of course devote more than this. Nevertheless, the GKR budget allocated proportionately less for the health during the war than the Sihanouk government had spent in peacetime. The percentage varied from 2.6 percent in fiscal year 1971 to 2.8 percent in 1974.[68] In a country with a desperate need for preventive medicine in order to avoid epidemics, the GKR spent a meager $185,000 on preventive medicine in 1973 and less than half that in 1974.[69] Moreover, in a country in which approximately 25 percent of the medical equipment was rendered inoperative during the war, and where there was never enough medicine and laboratory equipment, the total spent on both these aspects of the medical budget for government hospitals was only $600,000 in 1973 and $333,000 in 1974.[70]

Another result of this puny medical budget was that the government could not count on the services of its doctors for more than a few hours a week. Pay for physicians was so low (the equivalent of about $15 per month as of September 1974) and private practice so lucrative (up to $500 per month) that virtually all doctors spent an average of less than an hour a day at government hospitals.[71] The total number of physicians and health officers decreased in the first eighteen months of the war by 20 percent, while the number of nurses dropped in the same period by 42 percent.[72] Furthermore, the GKR's nonsupport of the health system resulted in the introduction of profit considerations into all medical treatment. The Steinbachs cite the case of the soldier Sirath, severely burned in an explosion, whose mother had to pay 30,000 riels to ensure his hospitalization and then had to care for him herself, bringing in food and paying additional for all medicines.[73] Whenever there was a large battle, a heavy influx of war wounded would descend on Phnom Penh—since there was no adequate system of military hospitals—to lie in the corridors without treatment, sometimes for days on end. By the end of the war, in fact, Phnom Penh was officially reported to have exactly 3,526 hospital beds for the city's nearly 3 million civilians, and this not including the military's wounded.[74] Dr. French described the "rather nauseating situation" that he found in a Phnom Penh hospital after a battle at Kompong Chhnang: "We walked down corridors with stretchers of men with open wounds unattended, filth and detritus, flies and insects and everything there, and there was obviously no medical personnel to meet their needs as yet."[75] A report by the Inspector-General of Foreign Assistance gives us a further glimpse of these conditions:

> The facilities were not only overcrowded; for the most part they were crude and unsanitary. There was an acute shortage of medicines and drugs. Death frequently resulted from infection and lack of proper care; medication was not being administered to patients suffering severed limbs or gross traumatic abdominal wounds. Little or inadequate antibiotic therapy was being given to patients in need of such therapy.[76]

The report described rooms in which as many as thirty were crowded into a space that could comfortably accommodate no more than three: "Patients overflowed the wards and were lying on mats or stretchers in the halls and corridors, their unattended wounds exposed to the dirt and filth of aseptic conditions; the stink of pus and infection mingled with the foul odor from clogged, flooded toilets." Sanitary fixtures overflowed into the hallways and were left uncleaned. Once again they found "not nearly enough doctors to go around," and the critically wounded waited "long hours" to be treated. Hospital operating rooms were "crudely furnished, unclean and totally without sterile precautions."[77]

These were the conditions in the hospitals emptied by the NUFK. But the hospitals themselves were not abandoned: this was only a temporary measure. One of the first moves by the new government in the weeks following the end of the war was the complete rehabilitation of the hospitals, in Phnom Penh as well as in other cities. Hospitals were cleaned and made sanitary for the first time in years, and then gradually restored to normal operation.[78]

Nor were all the hospitals closed down, even temporarily. The one hospital in Phnom Penh that was considered to offer adequate medical care, the formerly French-run Calmette hospital, continued to operate without the French doctors. The first French doctor to reach the French embassy after being expelled from Calmette hospital told everyone that the hospital was abandoned and its patients forced to join the march to the countryside. But ten other French doctors who arrived later that same evening contradicted this report. "We have the impression that they are replacing us with their own doctors," they were quoted as saying, "and in any case, the hospital is functioning normally."[79] This was later confirmed by journalists and other foreign observers, who learned that Calmette was continuing to operate with an entirely Khmer staff.[80]

The NUFK Medical System

Finally, those who have condemned the NUFK for emptying out Phnom Penh's hospitals have failed to take into account that the NUFK had its own medical system, one that was radically different from that of the GKR and that was far better adapted to the conditions of deprivation in which Cambodia found itself at the end of the war. A high official described his government's medical care system in early 1972 as consisting of one or more hospitals in every province, a fully trained doctor for each district, a medical committee for each village, and two male nurses with three years of medical training for each hamlet.[81]

This medical system was under the direction of Dr. Thiounn Thioeun, who was formerly the dean of the Faculty of Medicine at the University of Phnom Penh and director of the Soviet-Khmer Friendship Hospital.[82] In 1972 it was known to include at least twenty-five doctors who had left the GKR zone to join the resistance, as well as a number of Cambodian veterans of the anti-French resistance who had studied medicine at the University of Hanoi in the 1950s and 1960s.[83] In addition, there were paramedical teams which each year received three months training and then served in the hamlets, teaching people the elements of hygiene and preventive medicine.[84]

Moreover, contrary to the impression left by the news media that the sick and wounded were left to fend for themselves, the NUFK assigned medical personnel, including surgical teams, to the reception centers outside Phnom Penh. PNLAFK soldiers told a Western journalist that one of their hospitals was located at Takhmao, which is fifteen kilometers south of the capital and had been taken over by the revolutionary forces a week before the end of the war.[85] The two Swiss nurses who were outside the city for several days during the exodus reported that there were nurses and a surgical unit at a pagoda fifteen kilometers south of Phnom Penh.[86] It is clear, therefore, that many of the sick and wounded were cared for in NUFK medical facilities and by NUFK medical personnel. In the context of the unsanitary conditions in the hospitals of Phnom Penh, this would appear to have been the most sensible short-term policy to follow.

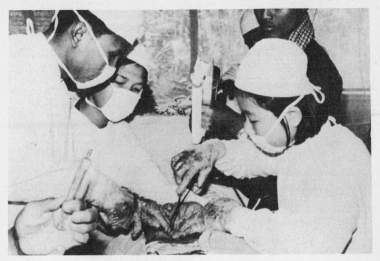
A NUFK rural clinic in the liberated zone, 1974.

The new government had to cope with the same severe shortage of medicines and other medical supplies that had plagued the GKR. A group of Chinese journalists who visited a field hospital near Phnom Penh in March 1975 described "an acute shortage of medicines and medical equipment." They found Dr. Thiounn Thioeun and his staff improvising substitutes for such basic materials as gauze, surgical cotton, and adhesive tape.[87] The NUFK received no significant medical aid from other countries, but, according to a former doctor in the PNLAFK, bought medical supplies either from FANK soldiers or directly from commercial outlets in Phnom Penh.[88]

In addition, the NUFK had its own pharmaceutical industry, partly organized early in the war by a leading Phnom Penh pharmacist, Mme. Khau Vanny.[89] In the immediate postwar period, the revolutionary administration organized the shipment of medicines from Phnom Penh to provinces in the north and northeast by boat, canoe, and junk.[90] Today the rural-based NUFK medical infrastructure produces seventy different kinds of medicine, including those for treatment of malaria and cholera, drawing on the great variety of local medicinal herbs, plants, and trees.[91]

In a population of nearly 3 million, in which hundreds of

thousands were physically weakened by starvation and where cholera had already begun to spread, it was impossible to avoid deaths during the evacuation. Contrary to the conception popular among American commentators, however, the authorities did avoid the massive death toll that might have been expected. Father Engelmann summarized the reports from Catholic priests who were among the evacuees as follows: "During the first days there were deaths: some very ill, some old people, some newly born— but very few. In any event, not thousands, as certain newspapers have written."[92] Moreover, to blame those deaths on the evacuation from the cities, as U.S. government political commentators have done, is clearly a case of misplacing the responsibility. Both the conditions that caused starvation and disease and the lack of adequate medicines were the result of U.S. policy in Cambodia, and not the fault of the revolutionary government. To have left the 3 million people in Phnom Penh would have invited a public health catastrophe of enormous proportions. The evacuation of Phnom Penh undoubtedly saved the lives of many thousands of Cambodians.

A careful examination of the facts regarding the evacuation of Cambodia's cities thus shows that the description and interpretation of the move conveyed to the American public was an inexcusable distortion of reality. What was portrayed as a destructive, backward-looking policy motivated by doctrinaire hatred was actually a rationally conceived strategy for dealing with the urgent problems that faced postwar Cambodia.

3

Cambodia's
Agricultural Revolution

In mid-June 1975, two months after the collapse of the Lon Nol government, a series of stories began to appear in the Western press with the common theme that famine was in store for Cambodia. They portrayed the food situation as serious, certain to become desperate, and made one frequently repeated prediction: that a million people might die from starvation over the following eighteen months.

For example, one article quoted "Western diplomats" as saying that "tens of thousands of Cambodians" had "already died, and are continuing to die."[1] At the end of June, U.S. officials told the Associated Press that Cambodia's food reserves were "in extremely short supply,"[2] while an article in the *Washington Post* asserted that "most people are said to be getting rice, the staple food, only two or three times a week."[3] A similar story in the *Philadelphia Inquirer* declared that "normal food is no longer available" since Cambodia had "ground to a halt."[4]

If events in Cambodia after the collapse of Lon Nol were treated as unfathomable by most of the Western press, there was no confusion about the origin of the reports. As the source for their assertion that "an estimated 1 million people are expected to

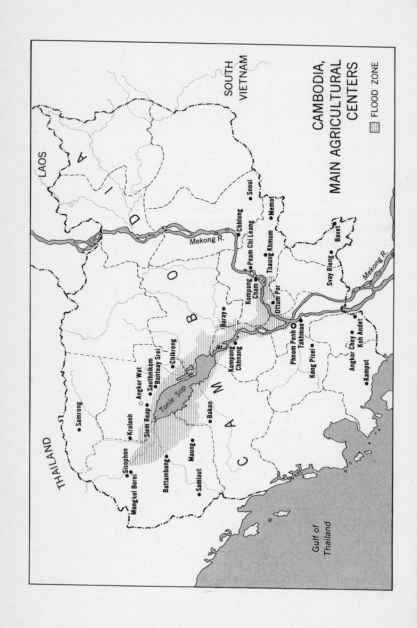

CAMBODIA,
MAIN AGRICULTURAL
CENTERS

||||| FLOOD ZONE

LAOS

SOUTH
VIETNAM

THAILAND

Mekong R.

Mekong R.

Gulf of
Thailand

Tonle Sap

Samrong

Sisophon

Mongkol Borei

Battambang

Kralanh

Siem Reap

Maung

Samlaut

Bakan

Angkor Wat

Sauthnikom

Banteay Srei

Chikreng

Baray

Kompong
Chhnang

Kong Pisei

Takhmao

Phnom Penh

Angkor Chey

Koh Andet

Kampot

Kompong
Cham

Ottum Por

Peam Chi Leang

Tbaung Khmum

Chhlong

Snoul

Memot

Sray Rieng

Bavet

die from hunger and exposure" because "food stocks simply aren't adequate," Jack Anderson and Les Whitten cited "an intelligence memo, prepared for the White House."[5] The *Far Eastern Economic Review*, a Hong Kong commercial weekly, went further: "U.S. Secretary of State Henry Kissinger has been actively leaking White House intelligence, including predictions that 1 million Cambodians will die in the next twelve months."[6]

These assertions were categorically denied by the NUFK in its official broadcasts and publications.[7] Furthermore, when confronted by a member of Congress who demanded documentation, the State Department retreated significantly, alleging only that "many thousands face the threat of starvation."[8] The Department was unable to claim that interviews with Cambodians who had fled to Thailand confirmed the existence of famine conditions, and conceded, in fact, that there were "many unknown variables, such as the availability of vegetables or other secondary food sources." However, the State Department did persist in its claim that it had "no indication of either large stocks of rice in the countryside or substantial foreign assistance to make up the deficit until the next harvest in December."

Neither the original allegation of imminent starvation nor the revised version rested on solid evidence; nor did they reflect the agrarian revolution being carried out in the Cambodian countryside. Although we do not have detailed agricultural statistics with which to formulate a precise estimate of Cambodia's food stocks, enough information is available to substantiate a very different interpretation. This information has been collected from a wide variety of sources, including Cambodian radio broadcasts (beamed in Khmer to a domestic audience and not designed for foreign consumption); scholarly investigations of Cambodian agriculture; interviews with Cambodians who left the NUFK zone or Cambodia itself; eyewitness accounts from foreign visitors; and reports from Western intelligence agencies. These sources taken together support the view that by the summer of 1975 the NUFK had successfully dealt with Cambodia's postwar food problem in the face of extremely difficult circumstances. As Deputy Premier Ieng Sary stated in an interview with *Newsweek*: "There is enough to feed the people. It is not abundant, but it is enough."[9] Since then, the evidence is overwhelming that Cambodia has moved from sufficiency to surplus.

The Traditional Rural Economy

To understand how far the new Cambodia really is from the starvation the U.S. claimed to see in its future, it is necessary to examine the working of the traditional rural economy before its reorganization. Cambodia is an agricultural nation and probably 90 percent of its population are peasants.[10] Before the NUFK began reconstructing the countryside, Cambodian agriculture was carried out on small plots and was considered the least productive in Asia. It was even admitted by an official U.S. publication to be "in a state of stagnation,"[11] with rice yields running only half those of neighboring countries.[12] As part of the French empire, Cambodia had been a victim of the usual "dual economy," wherein colonialism developed only those sectors that were of immediate interest to it. Thus, while in Vietnam the French focused on draining and canalizing the Mekong Delta to promote lucrative rice exports, in Cambodia only the profitable rubber industry was developed. The French invested virtually nothing—certainly no more than 2 percent of all colonial budgets between 1863 and 1939—in rice or other food crops.[13] By the second half of the twentieth century, Cambodian rice yields had not advanced significantly beyond those of 1900.

These conditions did not change after independence in 1953. On the most basic level, the tools used by the Cambodian peasants remained inadequate for the tasks of modern farming. The ploughs in general use "scraped" the soil, rather than turning it over, and rarely penetrated more than a tenth of a meter.[14] Without metal ploughs, and collars on the draft animals to which to attach the ploughs, the peasant was in effect operating with technology on the level of that of the early Middle Ages in Europe.[15] Worse yet, many peasants lacked even these rudimentary tools: of 685 peasants in 5 communes surveyed in the late 1950s by the French scholar Jean Delvert, 260 had no carts and 95 had no ploughs.[16]

The lack of ploughs was especially pronounced in rice-growing areas, where fully one out of every eight peasants possessed no means for turning over the soil.

Beyond technical inadequacy, however, the failure to establish control over the water supply was a major barrier to increased agricultural production. Figures given by Delvert illustrate the problem: from May to November an average of 1,218 mm. of rain falls. In the December-April dry season, this declines to 181 mm.,[17] and the rivers dry to cracked mud. In addition, the rains fall with considerable variation from year to year, frequently with disastrous effect. In Battambang in 1952, for example, rainfall was about 75 percent of normal. This 25 percent shortfall, however, resulted in the loss of 75 percent of the paddy in Cambodia's most important rice-growing area.[18] In a more recent example, cited by the International Monetary Fund, the 1968 harvest suffered a 22 percent decline due to drought.[19]

Thus the Cambodian peasant was "a slave to the climate,"[20] working on "a very narrow margin of safety."[21] Dependence on annual flooding and uncertain rainfall generally limited farmers to only one rice crop a year. Although management of the water supply was clearly required, Delvert observed that in fact "the Cambodian peasant carries on very little irrigation."[22] In effect, then, the traditional economy "relied on the sky" for agricultural production.[23]

Like most Cambodian economists and the NUFK today, U.S. officials also saw hydraulic management as the key to agricultural development. This was emphasized in U.S. AID programs during the Sihanouk period. Thus a 1959 U.S. AID report declared that "One of the government's major agricultural development projects is the improvement of irrigation facilities."[24] A principal AID project was the restoration of the Baray Occidental, the great western water reservoir at Angkor and one of the major hydraulic engineering achievements of the old Cambodian empire.[25]

Where successful, these irrigation projects increased yields between 50 and 100 percent.[26] The effort to build new irrigation works, however, was sporadic, and the results were negligible. From 1952 on, the amount of irrigated land grew at a rate of .2

percent annually, and covered a mere 3 percent of the total cultivated surface by 1974.[27] Few plans were actually put into effect, and fewer ultimately functioned. From the major U.S. project at Angkor, according to Delvert, "the peasants drew hardly any benefit,"[28] partly because of the failure to provide them with access to the stored water through a network of canals and ditches.[29]

Parallel to the lack of irrigation as an index of underdevelopment was the fact that the use of fertilizer was extremely limited. Peasants occasionally burned rice stubble for fertilizer, or used either the *antreang khet* weed, the detritus from green beans grown in the rice fields, or the water hyacinth that choked the streams as green manure.[30] But in general, according to a 1969 study by the International Bank for Reconstruction and Development (IBRD), application of fertilizer was "not widely practiced."[31] By the end of the 1960s, in fact, only about 10 percent of agricultural land was receiving fertilizer of any kind.[32] And had the amount used annually been equally distributed, each hectare (2.4 acres) of farmland would have received only 5 kg., compared with 800 kg. in Japan, 200 kg. in Taiwan, or even 50 kg. in Sri Lanka[33] (although Cambodia did use more than countries with very large populations, such as India and Indonesia).

The fundamental cause of the underdevelopment of Cambodian agriculture, however, was neither technical nor meteorological, but proceeded from the structure of the rural economy. To begin with, there was the problem of inequitable land distribution. In the six communes Delvert studied, nearly 50 percent of the peasants worked 1 hectare or less, enough with conventional yields of 1 ton per hectare to support an absolute maximum of four people.[34] Although tenancy was less pronounced than in other Asian countries, according to Western sources it had reached 20 percent by 1970 and was increasing.[35] Furthermore, the International Monetary Fund disclosed that it was "predominant in such fertile areas as Battambang," the country's major rice-producing province.[36] For tenants in such situations, rent frequently represented 50 or 60 percent of the harvest.[37] A growing number of peasants thus lacked suffcient land and cultivated the hectarage they leased under conditions far more beneficial to the owners than to themselves.

Since the rice market was organized by the merchants, small peasant producers had no control over the prices paid for their products. Each year at harvest time the peasants found that prices had declined, but they began to rise as soon as the paddy was sold. Should they later require seed for sowing or rice to feed their families, they discovered that prices were pegged at least 25 percent above the original selling price.[38] Furthermore, the government had the right to preempt a peasant's surplus at its own price. Since rice exports were the major source of foreign exchange, the government naturally sought the greatest quantity at the lowest price. Furthermore, peasants saw no benefits returning to them from the government. For a time the peasants were able to sell their rice illegally to agents of the National Liberation Front of South Vietnam or to Saigon black marketeers. After Lon Nol became prime minister in 1966, however, rice collections at prices one-third those offered by the Vietnamese were enforced by the army. These exactions and the brutality accompanying them were an important contributing factor in a peasant uprising at Samlaut in Battambang the following year.[39]

Moreover, tenants and smallholders alike shared a common burden: indebtedness. The weight of these obligations operated as a major drag on rural productivity, since past loans held a lien on future production. Delvert found that 78 percent of the peasants in Battambang were in one or another form of debt.[40] A 1966 survey of villages in Kandal province found that four out of five peasants had contracted debts during the year, and that 84 percent were still in debt at year's end, with the harvest largely completed.[41] By owing past payments to the moneylender, rent to the landlord, taxes to the government, payments for leasing a buffalo or plough or cart, and for rice to feed their families if necessary, peasants could quickly accumulate an enormous burden of debt.

"Six [riels] for five, twelve for ten" ran a common rural proverb,[42] and the peasant in difficulties normally encountered interest rates of 10 or 12 percent a month,[43] occasionally reaching as high as 20 percent—which amounts to a staggering 240 percent a year.[44] In most rural areas the local usurer was also a borrower, beholden to the major lender in the nearest town. The latter was in general directed toward the international economy, investing his profits in Hong Kong or Singapore, or else dissipating them in "conspicuous consumption" of imported luxuries.[45]

Nondevelopment thus had its own vested interests. For the large holders, secure in their ownership, there was no pressure from competition to induce them to modernize; they could in fact profit more from tenancy and usury than from improving production. Moneylenders, for their part, never needed to fear a shortage of clients, and at the same time had no incentive to reinvest in agriculture: their interest lay in a system of irredeemable loans, with the peasants forever saddled with the task of supporting the structure that exploited them.

The peasants would presumably have welcomed opportunities to expand production, but were in no position to amass capital for improvements. Chemical fertilizers, for example, were so expensive in relation to low paddy prices that they devoured most of the profit from increased yields.[46] Similarly, peasants in Sauthnikom commune in Siem Reap province obtained financing from five rich men (four of them rice merchants) to build a reservoir, but were obliged to pay half their crop in return and to concede purchase rights over the other half at depressed harvest-time prices.[47] Yet despite conditions so highly favorable to lenders, peasants in neighboring Chikreng commune were unable to interest local men of wealth in providing capital for a similar undertaking.[48] In essence, then, as Khieu Samphan concluded in 1959, "There is nobody to take the initiative for technical progress."[49]

Thus Cambodia confronted a situation in which the major producing class had no reason to increase production. These institutional barriers to development—including low prices and indebtedness—are in fact now regarded as the chief cause of the failure of the U.S. irrigation project at Angkor.[50] Circumscribed by a traditional social structure that militated against development, the Khmer peasantry gravitated to a level of production at which they consumed probably 75 percent of their paddy,[51] and rice culture, which occupied fully 70 percent of Cambodia's economically active population,[52] accounted for only 13 percent of the Gross Domestic Product in 1969.[53]

As a result, Cambodia's rice yields were remarkably low considering the fertility of the soil. Although in certain areas, such as Battambang, yields were higher, they were generally only slightly greater than 1 ton per hectare,[54] which made them among the lowest in the world: a 1965 study for the Phnom Penh government ranked Cambodia ninth in a list of ten rice-producing nations in terms of productivity.[55] In some areas yields were even lower: 600 kilograms per hectare in Kompong Speu, and in one district of Kompong Thom only 200 kgs. per hectare, or roughly three times the seed sown.[56]

Even more important, there had been no significant increase in Cambodian rice yields for fifty years;[57] production merely kept in step with population increases as new land was brought under cultivation. Between 1970 and 1975, in fact, there is even evidence of a *decline* in these already low yields in the regions controlled by the Lon Nol regime.[58]

The National United Front of Kampuchea (NUFK)

In this situation of rural stagnation and poverty, the NUFK rose rapidly—from formation to total power in a short period of five years. Two factors were crucial: mass participation by the peasants in the resistance, and the resolve of the NUFK leadership to bring about a revolution in the countryside.

On March 3, 1970, five days after Lon Nol seized control in Phnom Penh, the NUFK was established. Organized on a broad basis to include people from all social strata who were opposed to Lon Nol, it quickly became, in the words of one Cambodian diplomat, "the largest united front in the world—all the way from the peasants to the former king of the country."[59] In the countryside, immediate support was demonstrated within a week by the thousands of peasants who attacked government installations in Kompong Cham to the northeast of the capital and in Takeo to the south.[60] The Saigon and U.S. invasions in subsequent weeks, accompanied by heavy bombing, brought further peasant support for the Front,[61] whose influence developed steadily: after December 1971, with the failure of Lon Nol's last offensive (the 100-day "Tchenla II" operation), there was no further interference from the ground with the NUFK's consolidation of its rural base.[62]

By early 1974 one American analyst in Phnom Penh acknowledged to *Washington Post* reporter Elizabeth Becker that the NUFK had "built up a political and military movement amazingly quickly,"[63] and by the close of the year investigators for the Kennedy Subcommittee on Refugees assigned "less than 15 percent" of Cambodia's territory to the Lon Nol side.[64] A further index of NUFK control was the fact that Phnom Penh's exports, chiefly agricultural products, had declined 90 percent by the end of 1974 (measured against 1968 figures).[65]

The response from the peasantry can be measured by the growth of the revolutionary forces from between 3,000 and 5,000 guerrilla soldiers at the close of 1969,[66] to more than 200,000 by mid-1973, according to one U.S. intelligence estimate.[67] This mobilization was achieved partly through the NUFK's agrarian program (discussed below), but in addition by the patriotic appeal to the people on the basis of their tradition. NUFK cadre-training schools were conducted within Angkor Wat itself, and were thus permeated with the past achievements of the Khmer people.[68] Veterans of the anti-French Khmer Liberation Front returned to help organize the new movement.[69] Furthermore, the independence struggles of 1953, when 200,000 Khmers volunteered for paramilitary training in the countryside and whole units deserted the French forces, remained memorable as examples of popular patriotic resistance.[70] The Buddhist monkhood, largely drawn from the peasantry, also provided an important sanction, participating in large numbers in NUFK-sponsored conferences.[71]

The NUFK leaders were prepared not only to win the national liberation war but also to change the established order in the countryside. Their commitment was both to social justice and to development, or, as one NUFK broadcast expressed it, "to turn our beloved Cambodian fatherland from a backward agrarian into a modern agricultural and industrial country."[72]

The vice-chairman of the National United Front, Khieu Samphan—now chairman of the State Presidium—had worked directly with the peasantry for many years. As a student he called for programs to "fight to bring down interest rates and land rents."[73] As State Secretary for Commerce in the early 1960s, he had a reputation for austere honesty: according to a widely repeated story, at a time when holding a government post and owning a Mercedes were becoming synonymous,[76] Khieu Samphan lived modestly and his mother continued to sell fried bananas in Phnom Penh's central market.[75]

After resigning from the government in 1963, Khieu Samphan spent much of his time in the countryside, visiting each village in the Prek Ambel area, from which he had been elected to the National Assembly with 74 percent of the vote.[76] He made a point of spending fifteen or twenty days a month in the countryside, staying in the houses of poor peasants and attempting to reduce the debts they bore. In April 1967 he left Phnom Penh to join the developing resistance.

In addition to this practical experience, Khieu Samphan holds a doctorate in economics from the University of Paris. His dissertation, entitled *The Economy of Cambodia and Its Problems with Industrialization,* represented the first serious appraisal of Cambodia's relationship to the developed economic powers, especially France and the United States. He demonstrated that under the terms of Cambodia's integration into the West's free trade system, the undeveloped state of the rural sector was being preserved, while reliance on foreign aid and investment simply transferred abroad any stimulus from the purchase of new capital equipment. Thus he saw Cambodia's economic problems as stemming largely from its condition as "part of a whole whose center is outside the country, rather than part of a homogenous national whole."[77]

Other NUFK leaders have similar backgrounds. Deputy Premier Ieng Sary, formerly a student organizer and teacher, had worked

Cambodia's revolutionary leadership in the interior in 1974: Saloth Sar, Khieu Ponnary, Hu Nim, Ieng Sary, Khieu Samphan, Nuon Chea, Hou Yuon, and Son Sen.

with the peasants in the underground since 1963.[78] Two other leading figures, less well known in the West, are Saloth Sar, an engineer,[79] and Son Sen, director of Phnom Penh's Institute of Pedagogy;[80] they also went into the countryside in May 1963. Two well-known women leaders, Khieu Ponnary (head of the Federation of Democratic Women) and Khieu Thirith (now Minister of Social Affairs), joined the peasant struggle in September 1965.[81]

Hou Yuon, Minister of the Interior, Cooperatives, and Communal Reforms during the war, and Hu Nim, Minister of Information and Propaganda, have also had a great deal of experience in rural areas. When the 1967 peasant revolts against military land appropriation took place, both men left Phnom Penh for the guerrilla zones. Hou Yuon was largely responsible for the reorganization of the rural economy, and he, like Khieu Samphan, holds a Ph.D. from the University of Paris, where he studied the negative effects of usury and French credit policies on the peasantry. Hu Nim also has a doctorate, and his thesis analyzed the inequalities of Cambodia's landholding system.[82]

Thus the condition of Cambodia's countryside provided the impetus for the resistance struggle. Peasants long oppressed by the injustice and stagnation of the traditional agrarian system formed the core of the Front's forces, while its leadership was determined that—as Khieu Samphan expressed it in 1959—"there is no vicious cycle of poverty that cannot be shattered by conscious effort."[83]

The NUFK's Agrarian Reforms

Although the NUFK transcended class lines and was able to bring all elements opposed to Lon Nol and the U.S. intervention into the Front, its policy from the beginning was to view the poor peasants as the "main force."[84] The major changes introduced in the rural economy were designed to break the cycle of underdevelopment that was the source of their poverty. It is useful in discussing the NUFK program to keep two considerations in mind—history and necessity. In the first place, Cambodian society has always been relatively homogeneous in the sense that the majority of the people were small peasants producing in an essentially precapitalist economy.[85] Historically, all land belonged to the king; the idea of private ownership was introduced only in 1888 by Governor Thomson—and was bitterly denounced by Prince Yukanthor in a famous memorial at the turn of the century: "You have established property—you have created the poor!"[86] In fact, a dual system of property—actual ownership and rights derived from tilling the soil—continued into the post-independence era. The Samlaut uprising of 1967 was, in fact, fueled by the attempt of army officers to register and extract rent from land parcels cultivated by peasants according to this traditional practice.[87]

In addition, the Khmer peasantry have a tradition of cooperative labor. During the nineteenth century an extensive network of *prek*, or large canals, was constructed by rural communities. To carry out these projects, peasant leagues hammered out agreements on water distribution, elected leaders to supervise the work, and then dug the canals. These efforts benefited entire communities by providing access routes, drainage, and the neutralization of certain soil types.[88] Further, traditions of communal sowing and harvesting are still strong. Thus some of the important elements of the collective organization brought about during the war already existed in traditional society.

In addition, the violence of the war itself forced radical changes in the countryside. By official Cambodian reckoning, nearly 10 percent of the population of the liberated zone was killed outright, and the total of those killed, wounded, or permanently maimed surpasses 1 million.[89] The exigencies of a guerrilla war and the lack of medicine caused even more people to fall victim to malaria,[90] and photographs show the effects of salt deprivation.[91] At the same time, the peasants were driven off the land and into the cities.[92] Sixty percent of the refugees interviewed in one survey cited U.S. bombing as their reason for abandoning their homes; 40 percent mentioned shelling or ground fighting.[93]

To death, disease, and dislocation was added devastation—concentrated, according to the *Far Eastern Economic Review*, "in the richer part of the country."[94] In May 1975, twenty months after the cessation of U.S. bombing, Sydney Schanberg observed rice fields still "gouged with bomb craters as big as a swimming pool."[95] Jocelyne and Jerome Steinbach saw abandoned rice fields near Phnom Penh, incinerated sugar-palm trees, and bombed-out stands of coconut palms.[96] According to Phnom Penh's most recent assessment, several hundred thousand draft animals were killed in the rural areas.[97] The Swedish ambassador to Cambodia reported after a study tour that small communities in all areas of the country had been destroyed.[98] He added that, "One only needed to travel a few miles outside Phnom Penh to discover the deep wounds from the war. The United States had apparently aimed at destroying the Cambodian communications entirely during the bombing."[99]

But the chief result of the massive attack on the countryside was the irrevocable destruction of traditional rural society. The organization of the peasantry into an armed force effectively eliminated the former petty tyrannies of rent and usury, but previous forms of work and production had to be replaced as well. Individual small-scale production proved inadequate to meet the demands of the struggle, forcing the peasants to adopt new forms of organization that boosted productivity and guaranteed survival. As a leading Cambodian diplomat explained in the fall of 1975, "We could develop production because the agrarian structure—all the old agrarian structure—was destroyed in the war."[100]

The NUFK began to introduce basic agrarian reforms in 1970 and 1971. According to an interview given by Ieng Sary at the beginning of 1972, the Front had instituted sweeping reductions of rent and indebtedness in the first phase of the reform.[101] It also attempted to bring together land-poor peasants and untilled hectarage. The land of pro-Lon Nol absentee owners was seized and assigned to those who needed it, and the excess land owned by patriotic landlords was rented to landless or poor peasants at nominal rates.[102] Next, in a country where a number of areas had soil that was "poor or very poor,"[103] so that up to one-sixth of the land had customarily been left fallow to restore its fertility,[104] the NUFK began a campaign to promote the use of animal and green manure.

The relatively unproductive character of agricultural labor was another problem. Traditionally, each hectare required about sixty days' labor a year, and 80 percent of Cambodian families owned under two hectares.[105] Largely due to the impossibility of growing rice during the dry season, the Khmer peasant thus worked only about 180 days a year at farming and related tasks.[106] Furthermore, by 1970 there were some 70,000 monks,[107] mendicants who had to be supported by the rest of the population. Most young men spent some time in the monkhood, and therefore, as Delvert pointed out, "One peasant in ten or thereabouts is economically unproductive."[108]

The NUFK began to reorganize agricultural work early in the resistance struggle, initially emphasizing cooperative work and mutual-aid teams.[109] Beginning in 1972, however, the Front began to organize "groups of solidarity for increasing production" (*krom samaki bangkar bankaoeut phal*).[110] Angkor Chey, in Takeo province, which was liberated in 1972, established production solidarity groups at the beginning of 1973.[111] Ottum Por, in Kompong Cham, instituted them at the close of 1973 and the beginning of 1974.[112] Replacing a system in which farming had been essentially a family undertaking,[113] the production solidarity groups became the basic unit of agricultural work. They were in

Building a dam at Kompong Chrey, 1974.

turn organized into 30,000 agricultural cooperatives.[114] Although the peasants cultivate small gardens for their fruit and vegetables, today private property in land basically does not exist.[115] At the same time, agriculture has become a full-time occupation; in the production solidarity groups, workers debate options, carry out assignments, and shift to other tasks when the job at hand has been completed. Cooperatives may also decide to send peasants to work on a neighboring cooperative when labor is short, expecting assistance in return later on.[116] As one *Washington Post* reporter concluded after talking with people from the NUFK zone in 1974, "Work gangs are organized according to tasks instead of along the traditional, more informal family lines."[117]

The production solidarity group system treats people without distinction: "Everyone must work," as one peasant put it.[118] Monks, like the rest of the population, carry out productive work, digging ditches, tending animals, or raising vegetables.[119] Although this constitutes a major departure from tradition, given the needs of Cambodian society it cannot fairly be represented as religious persecution. Older people remain productive by weaving, weeding crops, or minding children.[120] Disabled veterans also contribute by guarding the rice crop against animals, birds, insects, and crabs.[121] Children, who customarily spend half the day in

Peasants applauding the completion of a water conservation project, 1975.

school, also work part-time herding buffalo or repairing crab holes in the rice-field dikes.[122]

Thus, from a situation of classic hidden unemployment and underemployment, labor power in the NUFK zone has been mobilized to overcome rural underdevelopment. The success of the NUFK program has been acknowledged by at least some of its opponents: a 1974 State Department report from Can Tho, South Vietnam, described the NUFK's reorganization policies and the introduction of new technology in nearby Svay Rieng province, concluding, "As a result, production has outstripped previous individual efforts."[123]

Water, Rice, and the Cambodian War

The NUFK's agricultural reorganization contributed directly to its April 1975 victory. In large measure this was due to the most important material change introduced in the countryside: the control of water resources. The overall objective was nothing less than the total transformation of the traditional agricultural cycle: by storing water and releasing it in periods of shortage, two and even three crops a year would become possible.

Programs intended to effect the mastery over water—
machhaskar loeu toeuk—were adopted relatively early in the
struggle. In January 1972 Ieng Sary referred to efforts to promote
irrigation in the NUFK zone,[124] and that same year, Snuol, in
Kratie province, used newly established production solidarity
groups almost entirely to construct water-management installations.[125]

However, the onslaughts of the U.S. bombing in 1973 interrupted the phased development of the water conservancy campaign. After the signing of the Paris Agreement in January, every
available B-52 in Southeast Asia was thrown into the
war. Up to 240 B-52 raids a day dropped at least 250,000 tons of
bombs on Cambodia in the most intense U.S. bombing thus
far.[126] A partial tabulation included in a Senate Foreign Relations
Committee Staff report discloses that nearly half of this bombing
was directed at Cambodia's heavily populated heartland.[127] Furthermore, the use of anti-personnel cluster bombs was documented
in dispatches by *Christian Science Monitor* reporter Daniel
Southerland.[128]

NUFK statistics record 200,000 casualties from this period of
the escalated air war alone.[129]

For 195 days, from February through August 1973, the heavy
attacks continued relentlessly. The incessant barrage prevented the
construction of water-storage facilities in many districts, thus
delaying the expansion of dry season rice cultivation. As a result,
both civilians and soldiers suffered from hunger. In September
1975 Ieng Sary alluded to the privation "during the difficult time
when bombs dropped all over, when there was a shortage of
food."[130] A delegation of Chinese journalists that visited Kampot
in 1975 also reported that "before 1974, the people here ran short
of food, and supplies for the army were also very tight."[131]

When the U.S. bombing finally ceased, however, the water conservancy program was extended "on an accelerated footing."[132]
Under the slogan, "In farming rely on the people and not on
heaven,"[133] hundreds of thousands of people in production
solidarity groups around the country began to build dikes and
dams, reservoirs and ponds, canals and ditches with feverish in-

tensity. At Bakan in Pursat province, one of the most important rice-growing areas, more than two hundred dikes were constructed between 1973 and 1975.[134] At Angkor Chey, also a populous rice-growing area, production solidarity groups worked "day and night" digging canals during the 1974 campaign.[135]

In general, the campaign met its objectives. Khieu Samphan announced, in a statement reprinted in *Le Monde Diplomatique* in November 1974, that following the "victorious struggle to harness water . . . two rice harvests per year have been generalized, and the number of regions that are able to get in three harvests a year is on the increase."[136] This was the first widespread dry season production of rice in Cambodia in nearly six hundred years.* As an indication of what this meant for one locality, Tbaung Khmum in Kompong Cham province constructed reservoirs sufficient to irrigate 544 hectares in the dry season, as well as another 250 newly cleared hectares.[137] As a result, the 1974 dry season harvest was 68 percent of previous monsoon season yields.[138]

The importance of the water conservancy campaign is reflected in two sharply opposing views of the 1974 harvest. An AID report dated October 31, 1974, betrayed anxiety about yields in the Lon Nol areas, partly as a result of the effects of war, "but also due to a drought that has occurred in the northwest of Cambodia" (the major rice-producing area).[139] Similarly, an International Monetary Fund study dated November 27, 1974, noted Phnom Penh's expectations of securing a harvest of 493,000 tons (about 20 percent of normal), but added, "This estimate appears optimistic as heavy rains after a period of drought have reportedly affected standing crops in some areas."[140]

By contrast, the Kampuchea Information Agency's publication *Cambodia—News in Brief* reported the situation, at almost the same time, in the following words:

---

* When the Chinese traveler Chou Ta-kuan visted Angkor in 1296, he found the peasants cultivating two and three crops a year, which was possible because of the well-developed water-management system. These rice crops in turn were the foundation of the power and prosperity of the old Cambodian empire, which then included South Vietnam and much of Thailand and Laos. In the following century wars with the Thai brought the neglect and destruction of the hydraulic system.

The people's masses and the groups of solidarity for production are building hydraulic works everywhere in order to search for and keep water. . . . Thanks to all these works in the liberated area in 1974, two rice harvests a year were possible and at some places three, and so in spite of the exceptional drought followed by serious strong floods.[141]

In May 1975, NUFK Radio issued its analysis of the 1974 crop:

The water problem is the key to our agricultural production: 1974 most glaringly brought out this truth. At the beginning of 1974 we had some rainfall, but by mid-year there was no rain. It was dry until the end of the year. Nevertheless, in 1974, we reaped a bumper crop which allowed our army and people to launch the final offensive against the enemy and win final victory on 17 April 1975.[142]

The direct relationship between expanded agricultural production, made possible by the water-conservancy campaign, and the NUFK's military success can be examined in the light of the fulfillment of the four main supply tasks that the Front faced.

First, unlike Lon Nol's FANK, no outside agency fed the NUFK. The liberated zone supported the PNLAFK, sustaining the last three dry season offensives entirely with its own resources. The responsibility for victualing the troops was well understood and was summarized in the slogan, "One makes war with rice and to make rice one must have water."[143] After the harvest, consignments of rice were sent to the front; some production solidarity groups in Kratie province, for example, were able to contribute 50,000 pounds of rice, with neighboring groups sending between 10,000 and 15,000 pounds.[144] American observers who had occasion to see "thousands of troops" in Phnom Penh and the countryside in the spring of 1975 reported that they "looked healthy."[145] Available photographic evidence from NUFK and Western sources confirms this impression.[146]

Second, the NUFK furnished sufficient arms and ammunition to keep the PNLAFK fighting. While a sizeable portion of the material needed was simply captured from the Lon Nol forces, NUFK agents also traded "a sack of rice for a sack of bullets" with Saigon soldiers, and once purchased the contents of "ten or twenty buses from Saigon" near the town of Bavet.[147] In a similar case, the *Los Angeles Times* reported in early 1974 that Lon Nol positions were being attacked with U.S. shells armed with a sophisticated fuse that had been made available only to Thieu's army.[148] During 1974 both Prince Sihanouk and Khieu Samphan were quoted mentioning NUFK rice exports to Vietnam, as well as to Laos.[149] The chief of the Royal Government of National Union of Cambodia mission in Paris, Ok Sakun, told an American peace delegation in April 1975 that the NUFK had traded some 50,000 tons of rice the previous year.[150]

Third, the NUFK was able to feed the population of the liberated zone. Unquestionably, conditions were extremely difficult in the early years. One *Washington Post* reporter spoke with a man who had left the NUFK zone with the complaint that "they take the rice to a central point and give you only a small amount per day to eat . . . we always had plenty of rice but we could never eat it."[151] (According to a peasant interviewed by David Shipler of the *New York Times*, about one-quarter of the crop was redistributed to the population.)[152]

The underlying significance of these stories, however, is that the NUFK "collected everything and put it in a common stock" from which all the various needs were met.[153] Supplying food was thus treated as a political responsibility and food was distributed according to rational principles. Furthermore, it is clear that the water-conservancy campaign and the effort to grow two rice crops a year immensely alleviated conditions in the NUFK zone. Whereas the situation prior to 1974 in Kampot province, for example, was described as "tight," the Chinese journalists' team was told early in 1975 that "both the people and the army had enough grain to eat this year and last,"[154] and Kampot today is one of the areas in which three rice crops a year are being harvested. A United Nations official who traveled throgh the countryside to the Thai border also commented that "people seemed well fed."[155]

Fourth, the NUFK dealt successfully with the problem of refugees from the Lon Nol enclaves. From the early years of the war it had been NUFK policy to encourage people to come to the liberated zone. In the spring of 1972, when French journalist Serge Thion visited the NUFK area for *Le Monde*, he recorded this slogan at a large rally in Kompong Cham province: "Let us enlarge the liberated zone and bring our brothers to live with us."[156] In a November 1973 broadcast, Khieu Samphan spoke of "encouraging more inhabitants who live in areas under temporary enemy control to come and settle down in the liberated zone."[157] At the end of 1973 *New York Times* reporter Shipler observed that "in the absence of American bombing, some Cambodian refugees have begun to filter back into territory and villages controlled by the insurgents."[158] In November 1974 Kampuchea Information Agency (KIA) indicated that preparations were underway to receive the "hundreds of thousands of inhabitants who will defect from areas under temporary enemy control in the dry season."[159] By the close of 1974, according to the KIA, some 40,000 people had already crossed into the liberated zone during that year.[160] During 1975 the exodus increased, and in January, the first month of the dry season offensive, more than 12,000 people entered the NUFK zone in the area around national highway Route 1 alone, with an additional 13,000 arriving from Neak Luong.[161]

The NUFK earmarked specific communal stores to feed the newcomers and Khieu Samphan, in his November 1974 letter to the Khmer people, referred directly to the NUFK zone's obligation to "help our compatriot refugees."[162] This policy was detailed in a 1974 Australian intelligence document: "Each village is required to establish its collective granary. Each family is required to contribute 20 or 30 kgs. of paddy for: (a) loans to the poor and refugees, (b) seed grain, and (c) feeding the troops."[163] Rice rations from these stores were later distributed to the people leaving Phnom Penh and other towns at the close of the war.[164] In July 1975, rice stocks were reported being moved from Battambang to other areas.[165]

Contrary to official U.S. predictions, Cambodia not only did not suffer mass starvation in 1975, but at the end of the year reaped its largest rice crop ever, and this was largely due to the effectiveness of the water-control projects. Without them, Cambodia would have been in the position of begging aid from abroad or suffering food shortages and privation.[166] With them, Cambodia was able to nourish the additional 3 million people from Phnom Penh despite the cessation of U.S. rice deliveries. That—not starvation—is the real Cambodian story of 1975.

Cambodia's Food Resources—1975

In addition to whatever rice remained from the 1974 wet season harvest, a major dry season crop was gathered in April, May, and June of 1975. In April, with the war still going on, one-third of the people in "N" village were assigned the task of bringing in the dry season rice.[167] In May, according to NUFK radio, the "entire northwestern area launched an offensive to finish off the dry season crop,"[168] and by June the NUFK announced that the harvest was double that of the previous year.[169] Samrong in Oddar Mean Chey province—never a traditional rice-producing area—reported that yields had increased 100 percent after the formation of production solidarity groups.[170] Thus, at the same time the NUFK assumed the responsibility of feeding the people leaving Phnom Penh, a substantial rice crop was brought in.

Nevertheless, the U.S. State Department was still claiming that it had "no information" that Cambodia was producing "two rice crops a year on any significant scale."[171]

Once the dry season crop had been harvested, the wet season crop was begun. According to the British Commonwealth *Rice Bulletin*, "plentiful rainfall" was reported at the start of the season.[172] From Battambang, all indications were that the crop was developing normally and would produce a good harvest. In June, NUFK radio reported that at Maung, which produces the highest yields in Battambang, the rice crop was "generally going well."[173] In July, Cambodians who had crossed over into Thailand reported "no shortage of rice seedlings" in the province.[174] In August, a Sri Lankan journalist who walked into Battambang from Thailand noted healthy green rice plants in various stages of development.[175] In Pursat province, considered

Double-cropping, August 1975.

the country's second most important rice-growing area,[176] rainfall
was reported "scanty" in some districts; with water released from
reservoirs, however, people were able to carry out their transplanting and had completed half that operation by mid-June.[177]

Beyond these indications of normalcy, there were also signs that
important innovations in food production were being carried out.
Although the State Department alluded to "the next harvest in
December" of 1975, as though no further rice would be available
until then,[178] it was clear from an examination of crop cycles and
of the varieties being planted that this claim was totally
misleading.

In traditional society, rice planting began around mid-May or
later, following the Furrow Festival in which the king performed
the first ploughing in the realm. In 1951 this occurred on May 24,
and in 1959 as late as May 26.[179] After the preparation of the soil
and the sowing of the seed, there was a period from one to two
months to allow germination, after which the seedlings were
transplanted. Due to the generally irregular rainfall in July and
August, the transplanting process was often interrupted and was
generally not completed until the time of the Prachum Ben
(Festival of the Dead) at the end of September or beginning of
October.[180]

Nevertheless, in a reflection of the officially inspired anti-Cambodia campaign, the May 1975 issue of *Newsweek* reported that "one month into the growing season, only 12 percent of the crop had been planted."[181] In reality, this item, based on aerial photographs, is proof that under NUFK leadership rice was being planted *earlier* than usual—despite the fact that April is the "most suffocating time of the year" and May is "not very rainy."[182]

Cambodian sources reported early planting in districts all over the country, such as Baray in Kompong Thom, Koh Andet in Takeo, Kong Pisei in Kompong Speu, Kralanh in Siem Reap, and Preach Sdach in Prey Veng.[183] China's Hsinhua News Agency team observed transplanting along the Mekong river in March, even before the end of the war.[184] By June 30 NUFK radio was able to announce—in Khmer to a Cambodian audience—that 50 to 60 percent of the transplanting for the whole country had been completed, considerably ahead of the traditional schedule.[185] The harvest, of course, was correspondingly advanced.

In addition to this acceleration of the growing cycle, NUFK policy, as explained by Khieu Samphan in early August, is "to grow quick rice and heavy rice at the same time. . . . to assure the life of the people in the immediate period and for the following year."[186] This policy is based on the fact that, among more than five hundred varieties and special strains,[187] there are three important types of rice grown in Cambodia: *srauv sral*—light or quick rice; *srauv kandal*—medium rice; and *srauv thngon*—heavy or slow rice *Srauv sral,* with light yields, ripens in four to six months and formerly comprised only 4 percent of the total national crop; it is also known as "tideover rice," since it ripens early enough to get peasants through until the main crop comes in. *Srauv kandal*, representing 60 percent of the crop, normally matures in six or seven months. *Srauv thngon*, making up the remaining 30 to 40 percent, takes eight to nine months to develop but has the heaviest yields.[188]

Srauv sral, or quick rice, if planted early, in April or May, would be ready for harvesting in August or September instead of later in the fall. In the spring of 1975, light rice was in fact planted in many areas in order to have enough paddy until the main harvest of *srauv kandal* and *srauv thngon* came in. In Pursat province, for example, Kornom district planted quick rice.[189] At Angkor Chey, it was planted toward the end of April.[190] Memot, in Kompong Cham province near the Vietnamese border, allotted two-thirds of its hectarage to *srauv sral.*[191] By early September 1975, harvesting of the quick rice crop was being reported, for example, at Peam Chi Leang in Kompong Cham Province.[192] A second variety of "tideover" rice was also cultivated on a more limited scale. *Srauv chamcar*, grown with slash-and-burn methods, was raised at Banteay Srei in Siem Reap province.[193] It requires little labor, yields are "almost always good" (up to two tons per hectare), and it matures by October.[194]

An attempt to promote quantity rather than speed can be seen in the experimentation with *pram pi taek*, a variety that produces up to three times the yield of even the heavy *srauv thngon*. With adequate water, *pram pi taek* yields up to 6.5 tons per hectare, and under even mediocre conditions it produces 3 to 4.5 tons. Where high-yielding heavy rice varieties were once cultivated, largely by rich peasants who could afford the risk of a long growing season,[195] *pram pi taek* is being cultivated on an experimental basis by production solidarity groups in every village.[196]

Another heavy rice variety, *srauv vea*, or floating rice, is also being encouraged. This strain normally flourishes in flood waters, where it grows rapidly enough to keep the developing grain above the surface. In 1975, Staung, in Kompong Thom, was able to plant 5,800 hectares with *srauv vea* because of the hydraulic system.[197] Chikreng, a district of 70,000 people in Siem Reap province, sowed more than 50 percent of its crop in floating rice.[198] Subsequently, experimentation with other high-yield varieties, such as *kramuon sar* and *champous kok*, has been reported,[199] while trial plantations have been established in Preah Vihear, Kampot, Siem Reap, Battambang, and Mondulkiri.

It should be noted that a number of other food resources existed in addition to rice. To begin with, corn, beans, and bananas have been emphasized by the Front since the beginning of the war: "In anticipation of a long war," Ieng Sary declared in 1972, "we attach great importance to subsidiary crops."[200] Corn *(pot)* is in fact now termed "our second production after rice," and "as much corn as possible" was planted in 1975.[201] Before the NUFK stressed its cultivation, only about 113,000 tons of maize were produced a year.[202] It is normally grown on the banks of rivers and canals, with the rice fields lying further behind, so that the two do not compete. In the early 1960s, about 75 percent of the crop was grown in Kandal and Kompong Cham, the most densely populated provinces.[203] Corn matures in ninety days and two harvests are reaped, one in March and the other in August and September.[204]

Green beans (*sandek bay*) are another important subsidiary crop. They mature in eighty days and produce between 300 and 400 kgs. per hectare. About 80,000 hectares were devoted to bean culture before the war.[205] Like corn, beans are planted twice a year, and are usually harvested at the end of May and again in September. Both corn and beans have been reported off-loaded and transshipped from Phnom Penh to other areas in Cambodia,[206] indicating that both form part of the country's centrally administered food reserves.

Bananas are also an important secondary crop. During the war they were frequently sieved and served as "banana rice," as shown in the Cambodian film, *A Heroic People*.[207] Banana trees do not occupy land that could be devoted to "our people's main strategic crop," rice,[208] and the trees can be chopped to feed swine.

In terms of protein sources, pigs are being raised at a number of locations, such as Srei Sophon in Battambang.[209] Errol de Silva, the Sri Lankan journalist who visited Battambang at the end of August 1975, reported pork was being eaten.[210] As more quickly developed meat sources, most villages are raising chickens and ducks as well.

Fish, however, is Cambodia's most readily available protein and remains the preferred source for most Khmers.[211] Its importance stems from Cambodia's peculiar geography: with the summer flooding of the Mekong during the monsoon rains, the volume of water deposited is so great that the river overflows into one of its major tributaries, the Tonle Sap, which then actually reverses course, flowing backwards to flood Cambodia's central plain for four or five months. The enormous volume of water expands the central lake seven or eight times, overflowing wooded areas and creating the *prey roneam*, or "flooded forest." The surging waters stir up the matter littering the forest floor, brewing a "veritable bouillon," "a feeding zone remarkable for its plankton," in which "fish have only to open their mouths to feed themselves," in the words of French commentators.[212]

As a result of this unusual ecological system, Cambodia enjoys the highest fishing yields in the world, up to ten tons per square kilometer,[213] or more than ten times the yield obtained by the North Sea herring fleets. One hundred and seventy-four species are caught,[214] and at least one, the *trey reach* or royal fish (a kind of catfish), frequently reaches a length of more than two meters, with a weight upward of 300 kgs.[215] The fishing season begins in November, when the flood waters start to recede. Much of the catch is eaten fresh, but the majority is preserved, especially in the form of *prahoc*, or fermented fish paste, which has a shelf life of at least two years.[216] Since the Tonle Sap fisheries were very little exploited during the war, postwar catches can be expected to be even higher than their normally high yields.[217]

The Cambodian diet did not lack other important ingredients. The restoration of national highway 3 from Kampot meant that salt from the maritime production areas became available.[218] In the fall, millions of *thnot*, or sugar-palm trees, began to produce a sap that can either be drunk fresh or converted into sugar.[219] In its assessment of the year since liberation, Hsinhua News Agency reported in April 1976 that both salt and sugar production had been resumed and that both were being distributed throughout the country.[220] Chiles and citronella (lemon grass) are cultivated along the margins of roadways.[221] Thus during 1975 the Cambodian people took steps to assure the continuity of their food supplies, and averted what in almost any other country might have developed into mass famine. By mid-summer 1975, Khieu Samphan was able to say of the country's food situation: "It is not an abundance, but we have been able to solve the essential problem,"[222] suggesting also that "in a year or two, there will be a surplus for export as well."[223] So successful was the food production drive, in fact, that by October 1975 Prince Sihanouk predicted in a speech before the United Nations General Assembly that Cambodia would "without doubt" resume food exports in 1976.[224]

The size of the first postwar wet season rice crop, harvested in the last months of 1975 and at the beginning of 1976, entirely bears out these assessments. NUFK radio described the harvest as "generally good through all the regions,"[225] while the *Rice Bulletin* called the crop "very good, apart from the south-west and west, where rainfall was lower."[226] Apparently relying on interviews with recent Khmer exiles in Thailand, the *Christian Science Monitor* called the harvest "excellent" and the *New York Times* pronounced it "one of the best in years."[227] Harvesting had barely begun, in fact, when Radio Vientiane announced that consignments of Cambodian rice were being sent to Laos to help alleviate food shortages in the new People's Democratic Republic.[228]

Official figures for the 1975 harvest, released in late April 1976, indicate that average yields have now reached more than two tons per hectare, or twice the prewar average.[229] In some areas results were even better: at Chhlong, in Kratie province, a high-yield variety with a short growing season produced seven tons per hectare.[230] For other areas, NUFK radio noted that Siem Reap province, once the granary of Angkor, had gathered in a "far more abundant crop than in previous years."[231] According to Hsinhua, "record harvests" were also obtained in each of the eight districts of Svay Rieng province—the area favorably reported on by the U.S. consul at Can Tho in 1974—"thanks to the series of capital construction projects."[232] A "good harvest" was also reported from national minority areas in Ratanakiri, Mondulkiri, Stung Treng, and Kratie.[233]

According to figures sent to *Le Monde* in mid-April 1976 by Thiev Chin Leng, former director of the port of Sihanoukville and a member of the NUFK residing in Paris, the 1975 crop amounted to 3.25 million tons of paddy, or about 2.2 million tons of rice.[234] For the Cambodian people this bumper harvest represents 250 grams of rice per meal per adult, and 350 grams per meal for workers on the production force.[235] These figures indicate that Cambodia has not only overcome the low consumption rates of the end of the war, but has also surpassed those of the late 1960s, when peasants deliberately restricted their intake in order to sell more rice on the black market in Vietnam.[236] Both allotments are close or equal to the 600 to 700 grams-a-day level recorded by Delvert in the late 1950s.[237]

In addition, meat eating has increased. In the past, under the influence of Buddhist tradition, the peasants took little part in the slaughtering of animals, and ate very little meat.[238] The NUFK has encouraged a change in this cultural attitude and is promoting meat consumption nationwide.[239] Today pork is alloted on the basis of one pig every two weeks for each production solidarity group of ten people.[240]

Recent visitors confirm these improvements in the Cambodian diet. Ambassador Bjoerk reported after a two-week study tour in March 1976 that he had detected "no signs of starvation," and had also seen "enormous numbers of children who looked quite healthy and quite lively."[241] Japanese journalist Mobuchi Naoki, who entered Cambodia illegally for a week in late April, stated that people "appear to be well fed and in good health." He stated that he ate rice, vegetables, a variety of fresh fruits, and chicken or fish twice a day.[242]

It is worth noting that as late as December 1975 a veteran U.S. foreign service officer with long experience in Cambodia was insisting that the NUFK "in their propaganda claimed to have produced large dry season rice crops. There was no evidence to substantiate this claim."[243] On the contrary, it is the officially inspired propaganda of starvation for which no proof has been produced. The evidence clearly indicates that the mobilization of the peasantry to construct water-storage systems has permitted an enormous expansion in food production. Equally clearly, the organizational capabilities of the NUFK and its centralization of food resources, tested by the war, have proven fully capable of distributing food stocks during peace. Thus the "starvation" myth has come full circle to haunt its authors.

The Future

Under the National United Front of Kampuchea, an undeniable revolution has taken place in the Cambodian countryside. The extent of the changes can be seen in the histories of two locations whose past and present are known.

In the spring of 1967 Samlaut, in Battambang, was the site of military operations against several thousand peasant insurgents who were protesting the seizure of their land by army officers.[244] During the repression hamlets were surrounded, inhabitants gunned down, houses destroyed, and a few hundred survivors led by Buddhist monks to safety in the forest. Those who were captured were executed with clubs "to save on cartridges," while the wounded were thrown from a cliff and left to die.[245] In July 1975, Samlaut's peasants, now organized into production solidarity groups, reported the completion of nine major irrigation projects, including a large dam, as part of the water-conservancy program through which they are reshaping the life of the district.[246]

In another district, Chikreng, in Siem Reap province, Delvert talked to peasants who wanted to develop water-storage projects but were unable to interest wealthy patrons in backing the enterprise; they were therefore unable to cultivate a dry season rice crop.[247] But in early 1975 the Chinese journalists' delegation that visited Chikreng saw fifteen thousand people building a "huge dam," and since then a 43-kilometer canal has been completed as a part of the district's development plan.[248]

These projects in two communities symbolize the physical and social transformation of the whole country. In a period of devastating war, Cambodia has taken the first steps toward agricultural development in centuries. The social institutions that held the peasants in subjection and indebtedness, and that discouraged innovation and the expansion of production, have been overthrown, replaced with a collective framework designed to release the creative energies of the people while at the same time allocating resources rationally. For the first time, peasants can see a relationship between harder work, increased production, and the overall development of the economy and the community in which they live. For the first time, as the NUFK points out,

"Our Kampuchea's people are the sole masters of their country."[249]

As an expression of this mastery, the NUFK has worked out a coherent, well-developed plan for developing the economy. Its guiding principles were expressed by Ieng Sary in an address before the United Nations General Assembly on September 5, 1975:

> After our total victory we extended to all Kampuchea the economic policy which had already been applied in our liberated zone. This economic policy consists of considering agriculture as the base and industry as the predominant factor. Agriculture supplies the raw materials for industry, which in turn serves to develop agriculture. Our objective is to make our country a modern agricultural and industrial country.[250]

The different sectors of the economy will therefore be closely related to each other. Capital raised by the expansion of agricultural production will finance both further investment in agriculture and the development of industry. As an NUFK radio broadcast put it, "The larger the quantity of rice we can export, the greater will be the possibility of importing machine tools, various engines, and other equipment for Cambodia's economic development."[251] In return, Cambodia's industries will produce the goods needed in the countryside as well as in industry.

The size of the 1975 wet season harvest makes such exports already feasible in 1976, as predicted by the Cambodian leadership in the preceding year. The 2.2 million tons of rice reaped in the first postwar years, less 1 million tons needed for domestic consumption and the amount needed for seed, will free for export five or six times the volume of the prewar period.[252] This year, according to an NUFK representative in Paris, water control will have been established over a total cultivated area of 3 million hectares.[253] In addition to careful seed selection, the use of natural fertilizers—compost, animal mature, river silt, ant-hill earth, and cave soil—is being encouraged.[254] These measures are expected to produce 5 million tons of rice for export in the near future.[255] Nor will there be difficulty in marketing this production: by late 1975 grain-short West African nations that had cultivated a taste for Cambodian rice during the period of the French empire were already inquiring about the resumption of trade.[256]

As part of the latest phase of agricultural development, the country has begun to campaign to consolidate separate rice fields into one-kilometer-square units surrounded by embankments and canals. These large units are to be subdivided by smaller canals and embankments into one-hectare sections, giving the country the appearance of an enormous checkerboard.[257] The intention of the campaign is to provide a more rational work area for agricultural production. Previously the countryside was carved up into small, irregular parcels—more than 3 million by the mid-1950s.[258] Since peasants did not always begin their crops at the same time, and since different varieties have different maturation rates, it was often difficult to harvest one field without damaging the crops in neighboring plots. The new canal system has canals wide enough to permit the passage of two boats at the same time and thus affords more convenient access to the fields. The system also makes possible a more organized approach to irrigation and the application of fertilizer, which can be controlled by section.[259]

Furthermore, the new system furnishes the basis for the mechanization of rice culture. This is a particular problem in the thinly populated northeast, where, according to a high-ranking Cambodian diplomat, "We need mechanization because we don't have enough people."[260] This program has already begun, with the reopening of the tractor-repair station at Mongkol Borei in Battambang.[261] At Sisophon, also in Battambang, sowing, pumping, and threshing machines are being assembled as well.[262] In other areas automobile engines are being used to pump irrigation water out of the canals, freeing the six or eight people who would have had to operate the pumps by hand.[263]

The enlarged field system will not be completed for two or three years, since rice production will continue in the meantime. Nevertheless, the results are already visible. Tunisia's ambassador, after an inspection tour in March 1976, commented:

It is correct that you should take agriculture as the main foundation for economic construction, and the solution to the water-supply problem is certainly the key question in the development of agriculture. The work-sites where embankments and canal networks are being built throughout the country are transforming the landscape of Cambodia. I am confident that in this field you will achieve success, with the admiration of the world.[264]

A stylized rendition of the field embankment-canal system appears in the new national coat-of-arms, adopted in January 1976. The networks are depicted leading to and sustaining a factory representing the country's industrialization plans.[265]

As far as industrialization is concerned, the first steps have already been taken with the reopening of Phnom Penh's industries. Of the 100,000 people now living in the city,[266] most work in the restored factories. For example, rubber factories at Takhmao and Chak Angre have resumed production, with the latter manufacturing 15,000 bicycle tires a month.[267] Textile mills have started up again at Phsar Tauch, Tuol Kauk, and Chak Angre, and by early July 1975 the Pochentong mill was spinning 4,000 meters of cloth a day.[268] At the Chak Angre battery factory, production is running at three times the pre-liberation output, and the new units are said to have double the life of the former product.[269] Enough paper is being turned out to meet government requirements and public information needs.[270] Foodstuffs, such as bean noodles and soy sauce, are being made in Phnom Penh.[271] The soapworks are operating at capacity, employing a new process that utilizes coconuts.[272] More recently, a locomotive-repair works has been established in Phnom Penh, and in April 1976 a new machine-tool factory was opened as well.[273]

While Phnom Penh's power plant, water works, port, airport, and numerous factories were repaired and initially operated by the PNLAFK,[274] new workers are now being trained as expanded production in industry becomes possible.[275] Other cities are also gearing up for production. For example, the rice mills in Battambang are operating, and a gunny-sack factory that uses Cambodian jute has resumed work.[276] Both the gunny-sack factory and Battambang's textile mills were reported in early 1976 to have attained production levels three times previous norms.[277] A phar-

Woman textile worker in Phnom Penh, spring 1976.

maceuticals plant has opened in Kompong Cham.[278] The Chakret Ting cement works in Kampot reopened in December 1975, "surpassing past levels" of output,[279] although it cannot as yet meet the tremendous demands of hydraulic construction in agriculture.[280] Altogether, nearly one hundred factories around the country have resumed production, all providing goods of obvious use in the agricultural sector.[281]

A second key element in the overall plan is the transport network. Despite widespread destruction and deliberate sabotage at the close of the war—railway rolling stock was bombed and Pochentong airport's control facilities were blown up[282]—the country's vital communications lines are being reconstructed. Rail transport is being emphasized as the most efficient for the country,[283] and the Phnom Penh-Battambang and Phnom Penh-Sihanoukville routes have been put back in service.[284] (On the other hand, forms of transport that consume gasoline are discouraged.) Mekong River traffic has resumed following the repair of ferry-ships and the dockside port facilities in Phnom Penh.[285] Most of the national highways have been repaired, and workshops have been set up to repair motor vehicles.[286] Prince Sihanouk's return to Cambodia in early September demonstrated that Pochentong airport was functioning once again.

In terms of more long-range development, the NUFK is currently taking inventory of all of Cambodia's resources. For example,
studies are being made of the rubber industry, where, according to
one American scholar, before the war yields per acre were the
highest in the world.[287] The plantations were nationalized in June
1974, and have since been reorganized. During the war, U.S. intelligence agents reported the exchange of NUFK-produced rubber
for gasoline from Vietnam;[288] now exports to automobile- producing countries are being considered.[289]

Studies are also being made of Cambodia's hitherto "little exploited" forests,[290] which cover at least half the country, with half
of that containing important hardwood stands,[291] including
mahogany and teak. Broadcasts indicate that the forests are
"regarded as a fabulous national treasure" that must be tended
with scientific planning.[292] Marine fisheries in the Koh Kong
region, formerly "little developed and badly organized,"[293] are
also being reorganized through the formation of production
solidarity groups.[294] In the past Cambodia exported 45,000 tons of
dried fish to Thailand and Singapor,[295] and the resumption of
this trade is planned. Possibilities for cattle-raising in suitable
areas in the northern parts of the country are being evaluated.[296]

In the NUFK's view, then, Cambodia today is sufficiently
strong to consider re-entering the international markets where it
once competed at a disadvantage. Furthermore, the changes in
Cambodia's economic organization make possible a much more
rational exploitation of resources for the benefit of the whole
country. This conscious planning carries over to the import side,
where, consistent with the principle of self-reliance, local
workshops turn out everyday home and farm items of bamboo or
metal salvaged from U.S. equipment.[297] In Prey Veng, for in-
stance, workshops have turned out 1,500 water wheels, 13,300 ox
carts, and quantities of ploughs and hammers in the year since
liberation.[298] In another example, a rice-hulling machine that runs
on rice husks has been developed by peasants in Sisophon.[299] In
this way earnings formerly expanded on plastic and aluminum
from abroad can be saved for domestic investment.

This conception of self-reliance, where the "decisive factor is

The coat-of-arms of Democratic Kampuchea.

human consciousness," is seen as the ultimate condition for Cambodia's development.[300] After the successful transformation of agriculture and the prosecution of the war to complete victory—by a country of but 7.5 million people, in an area the size of the state of Missouri[301]—there is tremendous confidence that major tasks of reconstruction and development can be undertaken and accomplished by the Cambodian people without outside help. Already on the local level this factor is credited with the restoration of the intricate textile mill machinery by workers who only a short time ago were farming rice fields.[302]

A high NUFK diplomat strongly emphasized the importance of this factor:

> When a people is awakened by political consciousness, they can do anything, they can study anything. It is very, very extraordinary—you cannot know about that. Our engineers who have French higher diplomas—sometimes our engineers cannot do what the people can do.[303]

In the course of the struggle since 1970, Cambodia has developed the political consciousness of its people, begun one of the most thoroughgoing agrarian revolutions in history, rebuilt much of the basic infrastructure necessary to a developing economy, and quickly resumed industrial production. Today it is carefully examining foreign markets for future export earnings, for which the natural wealth of the country provides a reasonable base. In addition, Cambodia has for the first time both a coherent national development plan and the organizational ability to put it into effect. The country appears confident that, in accord with the NUFK's overall aims, "a new Cambodia that is independent, peaceful, neutral, nonaligned, prosperous, having neither rich nor poor, will certainly be built in the very near future on the beautiful land of Angkor."[304]

Conclusion

The basic theme that emerges from an examination of the policies of two competing Cambodian governments toward the food problem is that only the revolutionary left in Cambodia had the will and capability to resolve that problem.

This study of Cambodia has shown that the ideology and organization of a society play central roles in determining whether its people will be adequately fed in times of scarcity. The Lon Nol regime was totally underwritten by the United States; yet, with the world's largest granary and the world's most advanced technology, the United States and its clients did not stave off starvation in Phnom Penh. The National United Front of Kampuchea, on the other hand, with only its own resources, not only fed its own people but also the more than 3 million people living in GKR enclaves at the close of the war.

This stark contrast in determination to meet the most elementary human needs clearly reflects the social and political character of the NUFK and the GKR. The Lon Nol side had no commitment leading it to assume responsibility for the prevention of famine, which was, after all, remote from the lives of government officials and the political elite. Their political survival depended on U.S. assistance rather than on meeting the needs of the population, and they were personally more preoccupied with the pursuit of wealth and luxurious living.

U.S. interests in Cambodia were defined by the narrow objective of keeping an anti-Communist regime from collapsing for as long as possible. There was nothing in the ideology of U.S. officials in Phnom Penh or in Washington which put the alleviation of starvation on a par with global political considerations. The United States was never willing, therefore, to divert money or manpower that could be used to support the war into help for the hungry and homeless. It refused to make the basic political decision that would have saved thousands from death by starvation. Instead, it opted for a continuation of the war, at any cost in Cambodian lives.

The NUFK, on the other hand, had from the beginning an ideological and political commitment to bringing about the development of Cambodia's economy and raising the living standards of Cambodia's people. Moreover, its military and political success clearly depended not on vast quantities of aid from abroad but on its ability to assure a minimum diet under the most difficult conditions. The NUFK was able to produce sufficient food only by adopting revolutionary forms of organization, which permitted the mobilization of the Cambodian people in the campaign to achieve control of water resources, an achievement completely beyond the capabilities of the old society. Then, through careful management of centralized food stocks at the village level, the NUFK was able to feed its people, its soldiers, and the refugees.

In the aftermath of the Cambodian war, however, the U.S. government had a significant stake in attempting to deny the NUFK's success in doing what Western specialists had predicted was impossible: avoiding widespread famine. Not only did implications of that success represent a threat to the whole ideological underpinnings of U.S. foreign policy, but the United States by contrast had been responsible for hundreds of thousands of deaths as a result of its war of destruction and the massive starvation of the cities. It needed to ensure that there would be a high level of moral indignation directed at the new Cambodian government in order to eliminate from public debate both the positive lessons of the Cambodian revolutionary experience and the U.S. government's own guilt for crimes against Cambodia. The evacuation of the cities was seen by the State Department as a golden opportunity to create an atmosphere of hostility toward the NUFK, and their comments, couched in the language of morality, thus had a far broader objective than simply condemning the evacuation.

What made it possible for the White House and State Department to shift the burden of guilt from its own shoulders to that of the new Cambodian government was the willing cooperation of the news media. Far from being impartial, the media's coverage of Cambodia reflected the interests and values of a society that remains unremittingly hostile to revolution. As in the past, the liberation movement was described as thirsting for revenge, careless of human suffering, and obsessed with control rather than with the welfare of the population. By contrast, the human cost of the old society, with its gross injustice, opulence amidst poverty, and needless death from malnutrition and disease, was forgotten. And the suffering visited upon the people by an imperialist power whose interests are confined to geopolitical advantages and exclude considerations of human life was also put outside the framework of discussion.

Cambodia is only the latest victim of the enforcement of an ideology that demands that social revolutions be portrayed as negatively as possible, rather than as responses to real human needs which the existing social and economic structure was incapable of meeting. In Cambodia—as in Vietnam and Laos—the systematic process of mythmaking must be seen as an attempt to justify the massive death machine which was turned against a defenseless population in a vain effort to crush their revolution. The lessons of the Cambodian experience, moreover, have a significance that goes far beyond Cambodia itself. We hope that they will not be lost to the American people in the rewriting of history that is already taking place.

Chronology

1945 October 5	French parachutists reoccupy Phnom Penh; Nekhum Issarak Khmer (Cambodian Liberation Front) organized
1951 March 3	Nekhum Issarak Khmer, Lao Itsala, and Viet Minh resistance movements form an alliance against French colonialism
1953 Summer	King Norodom Sihanouk launches a "royal crusade for independence"
November 9	Cambodia attains independence
1954 May 7	The French are defeated at the battle of Dienbienphu
July 20	Geneva conference ends; it orders free elections in Cambodia
December	Sihanouk declares Cambodia's intention to follow neutralist path
1955 March 2	Sihanouk abdicates as king, becomes chief of state

1956 Spring	Sihanouk rejects SEATO umbrella; Thailand and Vietnam impose economic blockade; U.S. threatens to curtail aid and begins to support anti-Sihanouk Khmer Serei ("Free Khmer"); Thai troops occupy northern frontier
1958 June	Diem's troops occupy parts of Stung Treng province; Sihanouk warned by United States to use U.S. arms only against "Communist aggressors"
July 13	Cambodia recognizes People's Republic of China
1959 January	U.S.-organized "Bangkok plot" to overthrow Sihanouk discovered and crushed
1963 January	Sihanouk nationalizes foreign trade and banking
May	Cambodia terminates U.S. aid projects; Ieng Sary, Son Sen, and Saloth Sar leave Phnom Penh for the countryside
1964 August 2	Gulf of Tonkin incident
1965 February 7	United States begins bombing of Vietnam
May	Sihanouk breaks off relations with the United States
1966 September	Right wing dominates national assembly elections; Lon Nol becomes premier
1967 March	Peasant uprisings at Samlaut in Battambang
April	Lon Nol launches campaign against leftists in Phnom Penh; Khieu Samphan and Hou Yuon leave for countryside
September	Hu Nim leaves Phnom Penh to join peasant struggle
1968 January	United States informs Cambodia of intent to adopt "hot pursuit" of Vietnamese forces across Cambodia's borders

1969 April	United States agrees to recognize and respect Cambodia's frontiers
May 2	National Liberation Front of South Vietnam opens embassy in Phnom Penh
	U.S. planes defoliate Cambodian rubber plantations; B-52's raid eastern Cambodia
June	Cambodian revolutionaries score local victories
September	Lon Nol returns trade and banking to private control
April 18	Lon Nol troops begin murder of Vietnamese civilians resident in Cambodia
	20,000 Thieu troops invade Cambodia
21	NUFK announces complete liberation of three provinces and partial liberation of three more
24	Summit conference in China includes Democratic Republic of Vietnam, Provisional Revolutionary Government of the Republic of South Vietnam, Lao Patriotic Front, and National Liberation Front of Kampuchea; discusses unity in struggles against the United States
1970 January	Army steps up attacks on Vietnamese liberation forces within Cambodia
March 18	*Coup d'etat;* assembly delegates, voting with color-coded ballots in front of General In Tam, depose Prince Sihanouk
20	United States recognizes Lon Nol; Thieu's troops cross into Cambodia
23	Founding of National United Front of Kampuchea (NUFK), with Sihanouk as chairman; formation of People's National Liberation Armed Forces of Kampuchea (PNLAFK)
26	Khieu Samphan, Hou Yuon, and Hu Nim join the NUFK; Khieu Samphan becomes vice-chairman

March 30	President Nixon, asserting that the United States has always "scrupulously respected" Cambodian neutrality, announces invasion; protests close four hundred U.S. colleges; six students killed, at Kent State and Jackson State
May 5	NUFK forms the Royal Government of National Union of Cambodia (RGNUC), with Sihanouk as chief of state and Khieu Samphan as vice-premier
May 26	Cooper-Church amendment passed by U.S. Senate forbidding direct U.S. ground support or advisory functions in Cambodia
August 10	NUFK announces liberation of 50 percent of Cambodia
October	Nixon administration trains Lon Nol soldiers in Laos to avoid contravening Cooper-Church amendment
December 31	NUFK announces liberation of 70 percent of Cambodia
1971 August 20	Lon Nol launches "Tchenla II" operation to conquer rural areas
December 2	"Tchenla II" ends in complete rout despite U.S. air support
1972 January 31	All eastern Cambodia liberated from Thieu troops
March-April	Prolonged student demonstrations against Lon Nol; three students killed
November 11	Sihanouk rejects ceasefire with Lon Nol
December 4	PNLAFK attack on Phnom Penh harbor
8	Tanzania leads movement to expel Lon Nol from United Nations
9	Khieu Samphan rejects negotiations with Lon Nol
27	*New York Times* reveals that one-third of Lon Nol's troops are "phantom soldiers" whose pay is pocketed by officers

1973	February 21	United States begins massive air war against Cambodian countryside
	March 21	20,000 students strike in Phnom Penh; Sihanouk begins tour of liberated zone
	June 29	U.S. Congress passes legislation to cut off bombing
	July 19	First National Congress held in liberated zone; B-52's bomb six miles from Phnom Penh
	August 15	Bombing halt goes into effect
	November 13	United States extends $700 million in aid to Lon Nol
	21	Nixon pledges ''all-out support'' for Lon Nol
	December 5	UN fails to expel Lon Nol by two votes
1974	January-February	Demonstrations in Phnom Penh
	May 15	Massive student demonstration in Phnom Penh
	November 28	UN again fails by two votes to expel Lon Nol
1975	January 1	PNLAFK launches final dry-season offensive
	April 1	Lon Nol resigns, leaves for Indonesia and Honolulu
		U.S. Ambassador Dean leaves via helicopter
		Phnom Penh liberated
		Special National Congress held
	May 12	U.S. ship *Mayaguez* seized in Cambodian territorial waters; crew released unharmed in advance of U.S. bombing of Cambodia's only oil refinery; U.S. landing force suffers 50 percent casualties
1976	January 8	New constitution adopted; Cambodia's official designation becomes State of Democratic Kampuchea
	February 27	U.S.-made planes bomb city of Siem Reap
	March 20	Cambodian People's Representative Assembly held to choose 150 peasant, 50 worker, and 50 revolutionary soldier representatives;

	all Khmers, regardless of their position during the war, are eligible to vote
April 4	Following elections, in accord with constitutional procedures, Prince Sihanouk and cabinet resign
	Khieu Samphan elected chairman of the State Presidium
April-May	Cambodia establishes diplomatic relations with most neighboring Asian countries

Based on information from *Cambodia: 1863-1965* (New York: Indochina Solidarity Committee, 1975); *Indochina, 1973* (Ithaca; Glad Day Press, 1973), and *Phnom Penh Libérée: Cambodge de l'autre sourire* by Jerome and Jocelyne Steinbach (Paris: Editions Sociales, 1976).

Notes

Chapter 1

1. P. Chabrier, H. Handy, M. Braulke, and I. Kapur, "Recent Economic Developments," International Monetary Fund unpublished confidential study, Khmer Republic, November 27, 1974, p. 5.
2. Ibid, p. 4; (1 hectare = 24 acres).
3. East Asia and Pacific Department, International Bank for Reconstruction and Development, International Development Association, "Report of Economic Mission to Cambodia—1969," October 12, 1970, vol. I, p. 13.
4. Chabrier, et al., "Recent Economic Developments," p. 5.
5. Ibid., p. 4. The crop year in Cambodia is figured from April of one year to April of the following year.
6. International Monetary Fund, "Report on Cambodia Economic Situation" (1970), in *Economy and Efficiency of U.S. Aid Program in Laos and Cambodia,* Hearings Before the Foreign Operations and Government Information Subcommittee, Committee on Government Operations, House of Representatives, 92nd Congress, 1st Session, July 12, 1971, p. 82. An IBRD report issued at about the same time gave the figure of 473,000 tons for rice exports in 1965—apparently an all-time high. See "Report of Economic Mission to Cambodia—1969," p. 13.
7. "Cambodia: CY 1974 Rice Supply and Distribution," prepared by USAID,

Phnom Penh, October 31, 1974.

8. Chambier, et al., "Recent Economic Developments," p. 2.

9. Until the end of the war, no one knew how many people there were in Phnom Penh, and estimates ranged from 1.2 million to well over 2 million. However, the NUFK, which took a complete census while dispersing the population of the cities to the countryside, discovered that there were nearly 3 million people living in Phnom Penh at the end of the war. Indochina Resource Center transcript of remarks by Deputy Premier Ieng Sary in New York, September 7, 1975.

10. Chabrier, et al., "Recent Economic Developments," p. 11.

11. Ibid, pp. 21-22.

12. Ibid., pp. 13-14.

13. *Washington Star-News*, September 23, 1974.

14. *Washington Post*, June 9, 1974.

15. U.S. embassy weekly economic reports, November 4, 1974, through December 31, 1974, declassified by the Department of State under the Freedom of Information Act.

16. Indochina Resource Center, interview with Norman Sweet by William Goodfellow, Phnom Penh, March 29, 1975.

17. See testimony by Assistant Secretary of State Philip Habib, in *Supplemental Assistance to Cambodia*, Hearings Before the Subcommittee on Foreign Assistance and Economic Policy, Committee on Foreign Relations, U.S. Senate, 94th Congress, 1st Session, 1975, p. 22.

18. *Chicago Daily News*, June 12, 1974.

19. Chabrier, et al., "Recent Economic Developments," pp. 13-14.

20. Jerome and Jocelyne Steinbach, *Phnom Penh Libérée: Cambodge de l'autre sourire* (Paris: Editions Sociales, 1976), p. 72.

21. Office of the Inspector-General of Foreign Assistance, Inspection Report, "Cambodia: An Assessment of Humanitarian Needs and Relief Efforts," March 12, 1975, reprinted in *Congressional Record*, March 20, 1975, p. S4619.

22. Chabrier, et al., "Recent Economic Developments," p. 15.

23. "Cambodia: An Assessment of Humanitarian Needs," p. S4619.

24. *Christian Science Monitor,* February 19, 1975.

25. Steinbach, *Phnom Penh Libérée*, p. 87. The authors report that Lon Nol replied to a delegation of teachers, "If salaries don't cover your needs, you have enough free time to make up for it; go fish in the river if you don't have enough to eat."

26. *Washington Post*, February 15, 1975; U.S. embassy weekly economic reports, January 21 and 28, 1975.

27. *New York Times*, February 26, 1975. The most authoritative foreign source on the Cambodian peasant says the average consumption of rice in Cambodia in the late 1950s was 600 to 700 grams per day. See Jean Delvert, *Le Paysan cambodgien* (Paris—The Hague: Mouton and Co. 1960), p. 154.

28. *New York Times*, March 11, 1975.

29. *Bulletin de l'Agence Khmer de Presse* (official GKR news service), March 29, 1975.

30. *New York Times*, March 11, 1975.

31. *Problems of War Victims in Indochina, Part II: Cambodia and Laos*, Hearing Before the Subcommittee to Investigate Problems Connected with Refugees and Escapees, Committee on the Judiciary, U.S. Senate, 92nd Congress, 1st Session, May 9, 1972, p. 30; Donald P. Whitaker, et al., *Area Handbook for the Khmer Republic (Cambodia)*. Department of the Army Pamphlet 550-50 (Washington, D.C., U.S. Government Printing Office, 1973), p. 92.

32. Comptroller General of the United States, *Problems in the Khmer Republic (Cambodia) Concerning War Victims, Civilian Health, and War-Related Casualties*, February 2, 1972, p. 22.

33. "Cambodia: An Assessment of Humanitarian Needs," p. S4618.

34. Ibid.; interview by William Goodfellow with Norman Sweet.

35. *Problems in the Khmer Republic*, pp. 22-23.

36. Ibid., p. 23.

37. *Los Angeles Times*, December 4, 1973.

38. Ibid., March 24, 1975.

39. *Humanitarian Problems in Indochina*, Hearing Before the Subcommittee to Investigate Problems Connected with Refugees and Escapees, Committee on the Judiciary, U.S. Senate, 93rd Congress, 2nd Session, July 16, 1974, p. 47.

40. "Cambodia: An Assessment of Humanitarian Needs," p. S4619. Another source reports a 24 percent average drop in the weight of Cambodian children between 1973 and the beginning of 1975. See United Nations Economic and Social Council, United Nations Children's Fund, Executive Board, "Indochina Peninsula, Relief and Rehabilitation of Services for Mothers and Children, Information Notes by the Executive Director," E/ICEP/L.1333, May 14, 1975, p. 11.

41. See Ancel Keys, et al., *The Biology of Human Starvation* (Minneapolis, Minn., 1950), pp. 128-29; cited by John Gliedman, *Terror from the Sky* (Cambridge, Mass.: Vietnam Resource Center, 1972), p. 52, table t.

42. "Cambodia: An Assessment of Humanitarian Needs," p. S4619.

43. Ibid.

44. Keys, cited in Gliedman, *Terror from the Sky*, p. 53; and H.D.S. Greenway in the *Washington Post*, February 21, 1975.

45. Dr. Gay Alexander, "Nutritional Trends in Cambodia," typescript, August 3, 1975, pp. 5, 7.

46. "Cambodia: An Assessment of Humanitarian Needs," p. S4619.

47. *New York Times*, February 24, 1975.

48. "Cambodia: An Assessment of Humanitarian Needs," p. S4619.

49. Ibid., p. S4620.

50. Dr. David French, "Report on the Cambodian Health Care System," unpublished manuscript, 1974, Appendix I.

51. "Cambodia: An Assessment of Humanitarian Needs," p. S4620.
52. Alexander, "Nutritional Trends in Cambodia," p. 8.
53. *Los Angeles Times*, March 24, 1975.
54. "Cambodia: An Assessment of Humanitarian Needs," p. S4621.
55. Ibid.
56. *Los Angeles Times*, March 24, 1975.
57. *New York Times*, March 18, 1975. This estimate is in line with the broadcast by the NUFK that between 300 and 400 people, "especially children and old people," were dying every day from starvation in Phnom Penh by the end of the war. NUFK Radio, June 30, 1975.
58. UPI dispatch, *Los Angeles Times*, March 3, 1975.
59. "Cambodia: An Assessment of Humanitarian Needs," pp. S4619-4620.
60. Ibid., p. S4620.
61. *Newsweek*, March 10, 1975, p. 25.
62. *Los Angeles Times*, March 24, 1975. For a recent summary of research on the damage to the mental development of children done by malnutrition, see Roger Lewin, "Starved Brains," *Psychology Today*, September 1975, pp. 29-33. Lewin points out that damage done to the brain by malnutrition in the first two years of life cannot be repaired even by normal feeding later on.
63. The problem of corruption was discussed openly at every one of the national congresses of Sihanouk's Sangkum party. See Laura Summers, "The Impact of Foreign Intervention in Cambodia During Its Early Years of Independence," unpublished paper, Cornell University, July 1970, p. 43.
64. *United States Assistance to Cambodia*, Hearing Before a Subcommittee of the Committee on Appropriations, U.S. Senate, 93rd Congress, 1st Session, 1973, p. 15; Comptroller General of the United States, *U.S. Assistance to the Khmer Republic*, October 10, 1973, pp. 55-56.
65. *New York Times*, December 27, 1972.
66. *Chicago Tribune*, June 26, 1974.
67. Ibid.
68. *Washington Post*, December 22, 1973.
69. Marcel Barang, "Cambodia: In Search of Peace," *Liberation*, July-August 1973, p. 15.
70. Ibid.
71. *Washington Post*, June 21, 1974.
72. Indochina Resource Center, *U.S. Indochina Report*, vol. 1, no. 3, "Cambodian Military Sure to Repatriate," February 20, 1970.
73. *New York Times*, March 8, 1975; *Newsweek*, March 10, 1975, p. 75.
74. *Baltimore Sun*, April 17, 1975.
75. Steinbach, *Phnom Penh Libérée*, p. 84.
76. *Problems in the Khmer Republic*, pp.10-11.
77. Testimony of Father Robert Charlebois, Regional Director for Southeast Asia and the Pacific, Catholic Relief Services, in *Relief and Rehabilitation of War Victims in Indochina, Part I: Crisis in Cambodia*, Hearing Before the Sub-

committee to Investigate Problems Connected with Refugees and Escapees, Committee on the Judiciary, U.S. Senate, 93rd Congress, 1st Session, April 16, 1973, p. 23. As an example of the lack of GKR interest in social welfare, Father Charlebois noted that there was not a single piece of legislation or a single program in the GKR concerning the problem of war orphans.

78. *The United States and the Rehabilitation and Reconstruction of Indochina*, report of Senator Edward W. Brooke, U.S. Senate, Committee on Appropriations, June 15, 1973, p. 15.

79. Ibid.

80. Indochina Resource Center, "Total Foreign and Domestic Resources of the Government of the Khmer Republic," chart based on official U.S. and GKR statistics, in *U.S. and Indochina*, no. 11, March 1975. These figures do *not* cover deficit spending as a source of income, which account for approximately two-thirds of the Cambodian riels used to cover the annual budget by the beginning of 1975.

81. Ibid.

82. See Indochina Resource Center, "Indochina War Statistics: Dollars and Deaths," *Congressional Record*, May 14, 1975, p. S8153.

83. Interviews with Cambodian refugees conducted by the General Accounting Office in 1971 revealed that 60 percent of the refugees moved from the countryside specifically because of the U.S. bombing of their area. See *Congressional Record*, April 18, 1973, p. S7812.

84. *Problems in the Khmer Republic*, p. 9.

85. Ibid.

86. Comptroller General of the United States, "Follow-Up of Problems of War Victims, Civilian Health, and War-Related Casualties in Cambodia," in *Humanitarian Problems in Indochina*, p. 156.

87. *War-Related Civilian Problems in Indochina, Part II: Laos*, Hearings Before the Subcommittee to Investigate Problems Connected with Refugees and Escapees, Committee on the Judiciary, U.S. Senate, 92nd Congress, 1st Session, 1971, pp. 71-72.

88. *Problems of War Victims in Indochina, Part II*, pp. 7 and 32.

89. *War-Related Civilian Problems in Indochina, Part II*, pp. 72-73. Peter Poole, "The Vietnamization of Cambodia," in the *Washington Monthly*, April 1971, gives a figure "over 1.5 million," while *Time* magazine used an estimate of "nearly 2 million," according to Senator Kennedy.

90. "Follow-Up of Problems of War Victims," p. 156.

91. Ibid., p. 157.

92. "PL-480 Shipments by Country," Agency for International Development, April 1974.

93. *Supplemental Assistance to Cambodia*, p. 13.

94. *Congressional Record*, April 8, 1975, p. S5400.

95. Information provided by John E. Murphy, AID Deputy Administrator, March 6, 1975, cited in *U.S. and Indochina*, no. 11, March 1975, p. 2.

96. *Supplemental Assistance to Cambodia*, pp. 11-12.
97. "Questions and Answers on the Situation in Cambodia, August 1975," p. 2, sent to Congressman Edgar by the State Department, August 13, 1975.
98. Ibid.
99. Associated Press dispatch from Phnom Penh, *Washington Star*, March 5, 1975.
100. Testimony of John E. Murphy in *Supplemental Assistance to Cambodia*, p. 26.
101. *Congressional Record*, April 8, 1975, p.S5400.
102. *Los Angeles Times,* March 24, 1975.
103. *New York Times*, March 18, 1975.
104. *Foreign Assistance and Related Agencies Appropriations for 1975*, Hearings Before a Subcommittee of the Committee on Appropriations, House of Representatives, 94th Congress, 1st Session, February 3, 1975, p. 12.

Chapter 2

1. "Cruelty in Cambodia," *Wall Street Journal,* May 15, 1975.
2. "Exodus in Cambodia," *Washington Star,* May 11, 1975.
3. Jack Anderson and Les Whitten, "U.N. Ignores Cambodia Death March," *Washington Post,* June 23, 1975.
4. William Safire, "Get Out of Town," *New York Times,* May 12, 1975.
5. Tom Wicker, "Revolution in Cambodia," *New York Times,* May 12, 1975.
6. *Newsweek,* May 19, 1975, p. 30. For other editorials along the same line, see "Cambodia's Crime," *New York Times,* July 9, 1975; Max Lerner, "A New Hard Communism," *New York Post,* May 14, 1975; "The Murder of Phnom Penh," *Chicago Tribune,* May 10, 1975.
7. *New York Times,* May 14, 1975; *Baltimore Sun,* July 25, 1975.
8. *New York Times,* May 9, 1975.
9. By the end of June, it was possible for the Associated Press, in a dispatch covering Henry Kissinger's remarks on Cambodia, to report as an established fact that the evacuation was "part of a campaign to rid the population of bourgeois tendencies." *Los Angeles Times,* June 25, 1975.
10. *Le Monde,* April 15, 1970. William Sullivan of the State Department testified in 1971 that only between 3,000 and 10,000 Vietnamese remained in Phnom Penh. See *War-Related Civilian Problems on Indochina, Part II: Laos,* Hearings Before the Subcommittee to Investigate Problems Connected with Refugees and Escapees, Committee on the Judiciary, U.S. Senate, 92nd Congress, 1st Session, 1971, p. 69.
11. Press communique of the Minister of Propaganda and Information of Democratic Kampuchea, Phnom Penh Domestic Service, March 30, 1976.

12. Long Boret, the GKR Prime Minister, said on the eve of the surrender that there was only an eight days' supply of rice remaining. Agence France-Press dispatch from Bangkok, *New York Times,* May 9, 1975. AID officials in Phnom Penh reported that the stockpiles of the rice would last only six days. William Goodfellow, "Starvation in Cambodia," *New York Times,* July 14, 1975.

13. See Ieng Sary's interview with James Pringle, Newsweek International Editorial Service, *Chicago Tribune,* September 10, 1975; Indochina Resource Center transcript of remarks by Ieng Sary at a reception in New York, September 6, 1975; statement by Ieng Sary, New York, August 30 (mimeographed).

14. Transcript of remarks, New York, September 7, 1975.

15. Interview in the *Chicago Tribune,* September 10, 1975.

16. The chief of the mission in Paris, Ok Sakun, told a group of American visitors in April, including one of the authors, that his government had received no foreign economic aid. For evidence that the armed forces of the NUFK obtained the bulk of its military supplies by capture or purchase within Cambodia, see testimony of Gareth Porter in *Supplemental Assistance to Cambodia,* Hearings Before the Subcommittee on Foreign Assistance and Economic Policy, Committee on Foreign Relations, U.S. Senate, 94th Congress, 1st Session, 1975, p. 121.

17. See the report by Sri Lankan journalist Errol de Silva, who visited Cambodia in August, in the *New York Times,* September 3, 1975.

18. This fact was noted by economists in Bangkok, as reported by Agence France-Presse. See "Cambodia's Move in Emptying Cities May Fill Food Need," *New York Times,* May 9, 1975. The article appeared, ironically, on the day that Schanberg's page one story was published in the *Times.* It was ignored, while Schanberg's interpretation was widely quoted.

19. *Chicago Tribune,* September 10, 1975.

20. This was observed by William Goodfellow, who was then in Phnom Penh as Research Director of the Indochina Resource Center.

21. As of mid-1972, before the massive influx of refugees reached its peak, only 35 percent of the population of Phnom Penh had access to running water. See "United Nations Development Program Report, Problems Posed by Displaced Persons Around Phnom Penh," in *Problems of War Victims in Indochina, Part II: Cambodia and Laos,* Hearings Before the Subcommittee to Investigate Problems Connected with Refugees and Escapees, Committee on the Judiciary, U.S. Senate, 92nd Congress, 2nd Session, May 9, 1972, p. 50

22. "Cambodia: An Assessment of Humanitarian Needs and Relief Efforts," *Congressional Record,* March 20, 1975, p. S4620.

23. Ibid. Also see the report by Agence Khmer de Presse (AKP), February 2, 1975, warning of cases of cholera in several districts in the capital suburbs.

24. Richard Boyle, "Exodus May Have Saved Cambodian Lives," *Colorado Daily* (Boulder), July 7, 1975.

25. Information provided by William Goodfellow.

26. Letter from Mrs. Sayhong Mabuchi, Tokyo, to Mr. and Mrs. Steven Heder, June 5, 1975. Translated from Khmer by Steven Heder.

27. Ibid.

28. *New York Times*, June 23, 1975.

29. Steinbach, *Phnom Penh Libérée* (Paris: Editions Sociale, 1976), p. 43. Phnom Penh Domestic Service, May 14, 1975, provides details on the sabotage of the Phnom Penh airport.

30. *Colorado Daily*, July 7, 1975.

31. Agence France-Presse dispatch, Peking, March 6, 1976.

32. Phnom Penh Domestic Service, May 8, 13, 15, 18, 22, and 30, and June 1, 1975.

33. *Manichi* (Tokyo), August 21, 1975. The return of factory workers several months after the evacuation was later confirmed by refugees interviewed in Thailand. See *New York Times*, January 21, 1976.

34. Phnom Penh Domestic Service, June 4 and 20, 1975.

35. *Bulletin d'Information*, August 24, 1975.

36. *Chicago Tribune*, September 10, 1975.

37. *Liberation*, October 13, 1975.

38. *Toronto Globe and Mail*, March 8, 1976.

39. Ieng Sary reportedly said during his stay in Paris in September 1975 that some 20,000 men organized into commando units were discovered in Phnom Penh. See Steinbach, *Phnom Penh Libérée*, p. 42.

40. Statement by Ieng Sary, August 30, 1975; transcript of remarks by Ieng Sary, September 6, 1975.

41. Ibid.

42. Ibid.

43. Ibid.; see also *New York Times*, May 9, 1975.

44. "Cambodia's Crimes," *New York Times*, July 9, 1975.

45. Jack Anderson and Les Whitten, *Washington Post*, June 23, 1975.

46. *New York Times*, June 23, 1975.

47. Ibid.; *Le Monde*, May 10, 1975; *Washington Post*, July 2, 1975.

48. Richard Boyle, *Colorado Daily*, July 7, 1975.

49. *Le Monde*, May 10, 1975.

50. Paul Dreyfuss, . . . *et Saigon tomba* (Paris: Arthaud, 1975), p. 351.

51. *New York Times*, June 23, 1975.

52. Ibid.

53. Dreyfuss, . . . *et Saigon tomba*, p. 351.

54. Steinbach, *Phnom Penh Libérée*, p. 40.

55. *Le Monde*, May 10, 1975.

56. Steinbach, *Phnom Penh Libérée*, p. 44.

57. *New York Times*, June 23, 1975.

58. *New York Times*, May 9, 1975.

59. *Le Monde*, May 10, 1975. The confiscation of automobiles was reported by

Agence France-Presse reporters Jean-Jacques Cazeaux and Claude Juvenal, *Washington Post*, May 8, 1975.

60. Personal communiction from Shane P. Tarr, Auckland, New Zealand, September 1, 1975. One Cambodian refugee in the United States has mentioned buses used to transport people from Phnom Penh during the evacuation. See Donald Kirk, *Chicago Tribune*, June 25, 1975.

61. Steinbach, *Phnom Penh Libérée*, p. 44.

62. See the testimony by Wells Klein in *Relief and Rehabilitation of War Victims in Indochina, Part I: Crisis in Cambodia*, Hearings Before the Subcommittee to Investigate Problems Connected with Refugees and Escapees, Committee on the Judiciary, U.S. Senate, 93rd Congress, 1st Session, April 16, 1973, p. 10.

63. Ibid.

64. Comptroller General of the United States, *Problems in the Khmer Republic (Cambodia) Concerning War Victims, Civilian Health, and War-Related Casualties*, February 2, 1972, p. 50.

65. Ibid., pp. 89-90. Dr. David French, "Report on the Cambodian Health Care System," unpublished manuscript, 1974.

66. *Newsweek*, March 10, 1975, p. 25.

67. See E.A. Vastyan, "Civilian War Casualties and Medical Care in South Vietnam," *Annals of Internal Medicine*, 74 (1971), p. 618.

68. *Problems in the Khmer Republic*, p. 47; "Statement of Dr. David French," *Humanitarian Problems in Indochina*, p. 49.

69. French, "Report on the Cambodian Health Care System," Appendix II ("Khmer National Budget for the Ministry of Health").

70. "Statement of Dr. David French," *Humanitarian Problems in Indochina*, p. 48; *Humanitarian Problems in South Vietnam and Cambodia: Two Years After the Cease-Fire*, A Study Mission Report, Subcommittee on the Judiciary, U.S. Senate, 94th Congress, 1st Session, January 27, 1975, p. 35; French, "Report on the Cambodian Health Care System," Appendix II.

71. French, "Report on the Cambodian Health Care System," section on Ministry of Health, pp. 2-3.

72. *Problems in the Khmer Republic*, p. 47.

73. Steinbach, *Phnom Penh Libérée*, p. 79.

74. French, "Report on the Cambodian Health Care System."

75. Testimony of Dr. David French, *Humanitarian Problems in Indochina*, p. 39.

76. "Cambodia: An Assessment of Humanitarian Needs," p. S4621.

77. Ibid.

78. Phnom Penh Domestic Service, May 23, June 23, July 7, 1975; *Bulletin d'Information*, June 20, 1975.

79. Lawrence Masurel, "Phnom Penh, L'ambassade en perdition," *Paris-Match*, May 10, 1975, p. 62.

80. Interview with a representative of an international organization who was in the French embassy compound after the NUFK takeover of Phnom Penh, August 12, 1975; *Colorado Daily*, July 7, 1975.

81. Ieng Sary, *Cambodia 1972* (Royal Government of National Union of Cambodia, 1972), p. 12.
82. *My War with the CIA: The Memoirs of Prince Norodom Sihanouk*, as related to Wilfred Burchett (London: Penguin Books, 1974), p. 199.
83. *Declaration des Intellectuels Patriotes* (Royal Government of National Union of Cambodia, 1972), pp. 23-27; Indochina Resource Center, interview by William Goodfellow with Lt. Mon. Chhen, Phnom Penh, March 8, 1975.
84. *My War with the CIA*, pp. 199-200.
85. *Colorado Daily*, July 7, 1975.
86. Steinbach, *Phnom Penh Libérée*, p. 45.
87. Chinese Journalists Delegation, "Cambodia: Self-Reliance Works Miracles," *Peking Review*, May 23, 1975, p. 12.
88. Indochina Resource Center, interview by William Goodfellow with Lt. Mon Chhen, Phnom Penh, March 9, 1975.
89. *My War with the CIA*, p. 190.
90. "Voice of the NUFK," June 2, 1975, in *Cambodia—News in Brief,* Office of Information of NUFK in Peking, June 5, 1975, p. 3.
91. "Voice of the NUFK" broadcast, July 1, 1975; Phnom Penh Domestic Service, November 26, 1975.
92. Dreyfuss, . . . *et Saigon tomba*, p. 351.

Chapter 3

1. *Philadelphia Inquirer*, June 17, 1975.
2. *Baltimore Sun*, June 28, 1975.
3. *Washington Post*, June 23, 1975.
4. *Philadelphia Inquirer*, June 17, 1975.
5. *Washington Post*, June 23, 1975.
6. *Far Eastern Economic Review*, July 25, 1975.
7. Phnom Penh Domestic Service, July 5, 1975; *Cambodia—News in Brief*, Kampuchea Information Agency, Peking, June 27, 1975.
8. This and subsequent quotations in the paragraph are contained in a letter from Robert J. McCloskey, Assistant Secretary of State for Congressional Relations, to Congressman Robert W. Edgar of Pennsylvania, dated August 13, 1975.
9. *Chicago Tribune*, September 10, 1975.
10. *Area Handbook for the Khmer Republic (Cambodia)*, Department of the Army Pamphlet 550-50.(Washington, D.C.: U.S. Government Printing Office, 1973), p. 263, says that 85 percent "lived in a conservative rural society"; Jean Delvert, *Le Paysan cambodgien* (Paris—The Hague: Mouton and Co., 1961), p. 32, using 1958 figures, estimates that 92 percent of the ethnic Khmer population is rural-based.

11. *Area Handbook*, p. 274.
12. David P. Chandler, *The Land and People of Cambodia* (Philadelphia—New York: J.B. Lippincott Company, 1972), p. 17.
13. Khieu Samphan, *The Economy of Cambodia and Its Problems with Industrialization*, unofficial U.S. government translation of 1959 doctoral dissertation, p. 33.
14. Delvert, *Le Paysan cambodgien*, p. 223.
15. Ibid, p. 235.
16. Ibid., pp. 479, 481.
17. Ibid., p. 36.
18. Ibid., p. 353.
19. International Monetary Fund (IMF), "Report on Cambodia Economic Situation" (1970) in *Economy and Efficiency of U.S. Aid Programs in Laos and Cambodia*, Hearings Before the Foreign Operations and Government Information Subcommittee, Committee on Government Operations, House of Representatives, 92nd Congress, 1st Session, July 12, 1971, p. 103.
20. Delvert, *Le Paysan cambodgien*, p. 651.
21. Chandler, *The Land and People of Cambodia*, p. 98.
22. Delvert, *Le Paysan cambodgien*, p. 224.
23. *Cambodia—News in Brief*, January 9, 1975.
24. United States Operations Mission in Cambodia, *United States Economic Aid Program to Cambodia, 1955-59* (Phnom Penh, 1959), p. 18.
25. Claude Filieux, *Merveilleux Cambodge* (Paris: Societe Continentale d'Editions Modernes Illustrees, 1962), p. 117.
26. IMF, "Report," p. 82.
27. Ibid., p. 106.
28. Delvert, *Le Paysan cambodgien*, p. 654.
29. Author's conversation with a Cambodian economist, September 10, 1975.
30. Delvert, *Le Paysan cambodgien*, pp. 118, 355, 415, 644.
31. International Bank for Reconstruction and Development (IBRD), "Report of Economic Mission to Cambodia—1969," vol. I, "The Main Report," October 12, 1970, p. 13.
32. IMF, "Report," p. 104.
33. Remy Prud'homme, *L'Economie du Cambodge*(Paris: Presses Universitaires de France, 1969), p. 73.
34. Delvert, *Le Paysan cambodgien*, pp. 456-65, 370.
35. IBRD, "Report," vol. I, p. 12.
36. IMF, "Report," p. 102.
37. Ieng Sary, *Cambodge 1972* (Gouvernement Royal d'Union Nationale du Cambodge), pp. 8-9.
38. Delvert, *Le Paysan cambodgien*, p. 516.
39. Ben Kiernan, "Khieu Samphan: Cambodia's Revolutionary Leader," (North Melbourne, Australia: Dyason House Papers, June, 1975), p. 7.
40. Delvert, *Le Paysan cambodgien*, p. 519.

41. Prud'homme, *L'Economie du Cambodge*, p. 83.
42. Author's conversation with a Cambodian economist, September 10, 1975.
43. Delvert, *Le Paysan cambodgien*, p. 517.
44. Laura Summers, "The Cambodian Liberation Forces," *Indochina Chronicle*, July 1972, p. 3.
45. Author's conversation with a Cambodian economist, September 10, 1975.
46. Delvert, *Le Paysan cambodgien*, p. 356.
47. Ibid, p. 363.
48. Ibid., pp. 331-32.
49. Khieu Samphan, *The Economy of Cambodia*, p. 29.
50. Author's conversation with a Cambodian economist, September 10, 1975.
51. Delvert, *Le Paysan cambodgien*, p. 360.
52. *Area Handbook*, p. ix.
53. IMF, "Report," p. 82.
54. Delvert, *Le Paysan cambodgien*, p. 360; Prud'homme, *L'Economie du Cambodge*, p. 67; IMF, "Report," p. 82; IBRD, "Report," p. iii.
55. Prud'homme, *L'Economie du Cambodge,* p. 75.
56. Delvert, *Le Paysan cambodgien,* p. 357.
57. Prud'homme, *L'Economie du Cambodge,* p. 75.
58. International Monetary Fund, Khmer Republic, "Recent Economic Development," November 27, 1974, p. 3.
59. Author's conversation with a high-ranking Cambodian diplomat, November 15, 1975.
60. Charles Meyer, *Derrière le sourire Khmer* (Paris: Librairie Plon, 1971), pp. 332-33.
61. See Richard Dudman, *Forty Days with the Enemy* (New York: Liveright, 1971), pp. 11-12, for a description of the anger encountered in rural areas by three captured Americans.
62. *Los Angeles Times*, February 4, 1974.
63. *Washington Post*, March 10, 1974.
64. *Humanitarian Problems in South Vietnam and Cambodia: Two Years After the the Cease-fire,* A Study Mission Report, Subcommittee to Investigate Problems Connected with Refugees and Escapees, Committee of the Judiciary, U.S. Senate, 94th Congress, 1st Session, January 27, 1975, p. 33.
65. *Far Eastern Economic Review*, September 20, 1974.
66. Ben Kiernan, "Khieu Samphan," p. 8.
67. *U.S. Policy and Programs in Cambodia*, Hearings Before the Subcommittee on Asian and Pacific Affairs of the Committee on Foreign Affairs, House of Representatives, 93rd Congress, 1st Session, May 9, 10, June 6, 7, 1973, p. 89.
68. Cambodian film, *A Heroic People*, 1975.
69. Wilfred G. Burchett, *The Second Indochina War: Cambodia and Laos* (New York: International Publishers, 1970), p. 71.
70. Meyer, *Derrière le Sourire Khmer*, p. 123.
71. Serge Thion, *Dans le Maquis cambodgien* (Paris: Editions FUNC, 1972).

72. Phnom Penh Domestic Service, July 11, 1975.

73. Khieu Samphan, *The Economy of Cambodia*, p. 69.

74. Meyer, *Derrière le Sourire Khmer*, p. 178.

75. Kiernan, "Khieu Samphan," p. 6.

76. Ibid.

77. Khieu Samphan, *The Economy of Cambodia*, 4.

78. Author's conversation with a Cambodian economist, September 18, 1975.

79. Forces Armees Nationales Khmeres, Deuxieme Bureau, "Des Mouvements Anti-Gouvernementaux au Cambodge," July 1973, p. 43.

80. Burchett, *The Second Indochina War*, p. 53.

81. FANK, "Des Mouvements Anti-Gouvernementaux," p. 41.

82. Summers, "The Cambodian Liberation Forces," pp. 2-5.

83. Khieu Samphan, *The Economy of Cambodia*, p. 117.

84. Ieng Sary, *Cambodge 1972*, p. 7.

85. Khieu Samphan, *The Economy of Cambodia*, p. 27.

86. Meyer, *Derrière le Sourire Khmer*, p. 203.

87. Author's conversation with Mr. Thiounn Prasith, Chief of the Delegation of the State of Democratic Kampuchea to the United Nations Conference on the Law of the Sea, May 6, 1976.

88. Delvert, *Le Paysan cambodgien*, pp. 388-92.

89. "Communique of Mr. Hu Nim, Minister of Information and Propaganda of Democratic Kampuchea, About the Ceremonies Commemorating the First Anniversary of Democratic Kampuchea" (unofficial translation), March 31, 1976, p. 7.

90. Author's conversation with a high-ranking Cambodian diplomat, November 15,1975.

91. Prince Norodom Sihanouk, Head of State of Cambodia, in the Liberated Zone, 1973.

92. *New York Times*, September 8, 1975.

93. *Relief and Rehabilitation of War Victims in Indochina, Part 1: Crisis in Cambodia*, Hearings Before the Subcommittee to Investigate Problems Connected with Refugees and Escapees, Committee on the Judiciary, U.S. Senate, 93rd Congress, 1st Session, April 16, 1973, p. 3.

94. *Asia 1976 Yearbook* (Hong Kong: Far Eastern Economic Review, 1975), p. 136.

95. *New York Times*, May 9, 1975. NUFK radio reported the reactions of some of the people returning to their homes from Phnom Penh: "What devastation! We never thought that there was so much destruction!" (Phnom Penh Domestic Service, June 5, 1975); "When we crossed Route 38, we felt extremely indignant: this was the first time we witnessed the immense destruction that the U.S. imperialist war had brought to our country. The U.S. imperialists owe immense blood debts to our people" (Phnom Penh Domestic Service, June 13, 1975).

96. Jerome and Jocelyne Steinbach, *Phnom Penh Libérée: Cambodge de l'autre sourire* (Paris: Editions Sociales, 1976), pp. 30, 96.

97. Phnom Penh Domestic Service, April 15, 1976.
98. *Toronto Globe and Mail*, March 8, 1976.
99. *Bangkok Post*, March 8, 1976.
100. Author's conversation with a high-ranking Cambodian diplomat, November 15, 1975.
101. Ieng Sary, *Cambodge 1972*, pp. 7-8.
102. Ibid., p. 8.
103. Prud'homme, *L'Economie du Cambodge*, p. 19.
104. Delvert, *Le Paysan cambodgien*, p. 355.
105. Ibid., pp. 347, 495.
106. Khieu Samphan, *The Economy of Cambodia*, p. 75.
107. Chandler, *The Land and People of Cambodia*, p. 112.
108. Delvert, *Le Paysan cambodgien*, p. 140.
109. Ieng Sary, *Cambodge 1972*, p. 9.
110. *Cambodia—News in Brief*, June 17, 1975.
111. Phnom Penh Domestic Service, June 5, 1975.
112. *Bulletin d'Information*, Mission du Gouvernement Royal d'Union Nationale du Cambodge, Paris, July 18, 1975.
113. Khieu Samphan, *The Economy of Cambodia*, p. 2.
114. Steinbach, *Phnom Penh Libérée*, p. 44.
115. Author's conversation with Mr. Thiounn Prasith, May 6, 1976.
116. Ibid.
117. *Washington Post*, February 3, 1974.
118. *New York Daily News*, May 13, 1975.
119. *Washington Star*, April 10, 1974; *Washington Post*, March 10, 1974.
120. *Bulletin d'Information*, June 27, 1975.
121. Phnom Penh Domestic Service, May 10, 1975.
122. Ibid., May 7, 1975.
123. U.S. Department of State, Report from the American Consul in Can Tho.
124. Ieng Sary, *Cambodge 1972*, p. 9; *Bulletin d'Information*, August 22, 1975.
125. Phnom Penh Domestic Service, June 7, 1975.
126. *Washington Post*, April 28, 1973; *Congressional Record*, July 18, 1973, pp. S13848-13851; figures prorated through August 15, 1973.
127. *U.S. Air Operation in Cambodia: April 1973*, A Staff Report, Subcommittee on U.S. Security Agreements and Commitments Abroad, Committee on Foreign Relations, U.S. Senate, April 27, 1973, p. 8.
128. *Christian Science Monitor,* April 24, 1973.
129. Phnom Penh Domestic Service, May 9, 1975; the 200,000 figure includes the categories of "killed, wounded, and crippled for life."
130. Indochina Resource Center, transcript of remarks by Deputy Premier of the Royal Government of National Union of Cambodia Ieng Sary, in New York City, September 6, 1975.
131. *Peking Review*, June 6, 1975.
132. *Afrique-Asie*, October 29, 1973.

133. *A Heroic People*.
134. *Cambodia—News in Brief*, March 13, 1975.
135. Phnom Penh Domestic Service, June 5, 1975.
136. *Le Monde Diplomatique*, November 1974.
137. *Bulletin d'Information*, January 31, 1975.
138. *Peking Review*, June 6, 1975.
139. U.S. AID Report, Phnom Penh, October 31, 1974, p. 4.
140. IMF, "Report," p. 5.
141. *Cambodia—News in Brief*, January 9, 1975; see also Phnom Penh Domestic Service, November 6, 1975.
142. Phnom Penh Domestic Service, May 1, 1975.
143. *Cambodia—News in Brief*, December 26, 1974.
144. Phnom Penh Domestic Service, June 6, 1975.
145. *New York Times*, May 9, 1975.
146. See, for example, *New York Times*, May 9, 1975; *Newsweek*, May 19, 1975; Pacific News Service, photographs by Richard Boyle.
147. *Chicago Tribune*, June 12, 1974.
148. *Los Angeles Times*, February 9, 1974.
149. IMF, "Report," confidential supplement; *Le Monde Diplomatique*, November 1974.
150. Author's interview, April 8, 1975.
151. *Washington Post*, February 3, 1974.
152. *New York Times*, June 19, 1974.
153. *Chicago Daily News*, May 11, 1974.
154. *Peking Review*, June 6, 1975.
155. Author's interview with a United Nations official, July 28, 1975.
156. Serge Thion, *Dans le Maquis cambodgien*, p. 14.
157. Phnom Penh Domestic Service, November 6, 1974.
158. *New York Times*, December 8, 1973.
159. AKI, November 6, 1974.
160. *Guardian*, December 25, 1974.
161. *Cambodia—News in Brief*, January 21, 1975.
162. Phnom Penh Domestic Service, November 13, 1974.
163. Australian embassy, Phnom Penh, "FUNK Policy and Organization," 1974.
164. *New York Times*, June 13, 1975.
165. *Washington Post*, July 13, 1975.
166. Recent international experience appears to confirm the NUFK's decision to rely on its own resources. In Ethiopia during 1975 some 500,000 people in the Ogaden area suffered drought and starvation, with casualties running into the thousands. Nonetheless, an article in the *Los Angeles Times* of July 13 quotes a relief official as saying: "The Ethiopians have cried wolf too often. There is a real wolf there. But we have to carefully consider each government request for aid." Subsequently, the *Washington Post* reported on April 29, 1976, that, "While the [Ethiopian government's Drought Relief and Rehabilitation] Com-

mission warns of a potential disaster and a chronic need to shelter 100,000 nomads in the southeastern Ogaden region, foreign relief officials read the signs differently—as they have in previous years. . . . The question of who was at fault for the death of an estimated 3,000 to 4,000 nomads in the Ogaden region last summer is an extremely delicate issue for both sides. . . . The Commission's latest drought status report comes in the wake of an article by British journalist Jonathan Dimbleby charging that international relief agencies and private groups . . . were largely responsible . . . because of their refusal to heed the government's spring warnings.''

167. *Bulletin d'Information*, April 18, 1975.
168. Phnom Penh Domestic Service, May 2, 1975.
169. Ibid., June 22, 1975.
170. Ibid.
171. Letter to Congressman Edgar, August 13, 1975.
172. *Rice Bulletin*, August 1975, p. 163.
173. Phnom Penh Domestic Service, June 1, 1975.
174. *Washington Post*, July 13, 1975.
175. *New York Times*, September 3, 1975.
176. Phnom Penh Domestic Service, May 21, 1975.
177. Ibid., June 18, 1975.
178. Letter to Congressman Edgar, August 13, 1975.
179. Delvert, *Le Paysan cambodgien*, p. 339.
180. Ibid., p. 342.
181. *Newsweek*, May 19, 1975.
182. G.H. Monod, *Les Contes Khmers* (Mouans-Sartoux, Alpes-Maritimes: Publications Chitra, 1943), p. 303; Delvert, *Le Paysan cambodgien*, p. 151.
183. Phnom Penh Domestic Service, May 30, June 14, June 23, July 22, June 2, 1975.
184. Hsinhua News Agency, May 16, 1975.
185. Ibid., June 30, 1975.
186. *Bulletin d'Information*, August 22, 1975.
187. Phnom Penh Domestic Service, December 23, 1975.
188. Delvert, *Le Paysan cambodgien*, p. 323 et seq.
189. *Bulletin d'Information*, August 5, 1975.
190. Phnom Penh Domestic Service, June 5, 1975.
191. Ibid., July 18, 1975.
192. *Bulletin d'Information*, September 5, 1975.
193. Phnom Penh Domestic Service, June 30, 1975.
194. Delvert, *Le Paysan cambodgien*, p. 365.
195. Ibid., p. 335.
196. *Bulletin d'Information*, August 15, 1975.
197. Ibid., August 22, 1975.
198. Phnom Penh Domestic Service, June 13, 1975.
199. Ibid., January 5 and February 6, 1976.

200. Ieng Sary, *Cambodge 1972*, p. 9.
201. *Bulletin d'Information*, September 5 and June 6, 1975.
202. IMF, "Report," p. 83.
203. Tan Kim Huon, *Géographie du Cambodge* (Phnom Penh: Imprimerie Ramsey, 1961), p. 106.
204. Delvert, *Le Paysan cambodgien*, p. 411 et seq.
205. Ibid., pp. 416, 372.
206. *Washington Post*, June 18, 1975.
207. *A Heroic People*.
208. Phnom Penh Domestic Service, May 31, 1975.
209. *Bulletin d'Information*, July 18, 1975.
210. *New York Times*, September 3, 1975.
211. *Area Handbook*, p. 272.
212. Pierre Gourou, in Huon, *Géographie du Cambodge*, p. 118; Delvert, *Le Paysan cambodgien*, p. 161.
213. Gourou, in ibid., p. 115.
214. *Bulletin d'Information*, August 1, 1975.
215. Filieux, *Merveilleux Cambodge*, p. 13.
216. Delvert, *Le Paysan cambodgien*, p. 151.
217. Author's conversation with Mr. Thiounn Prasith, May 6, 1976.
218. Phnom Penh Domestic Service, May 26, 1975; *A Heroic People*.
219. *A Heroic People*; Delvert, *Le Paysan cambodgien*, pp. 289, 293.
220. Hsinhua News Service, April 15, 1976.
221. Phnom Penh Domestic Service, June 20, 1975.
222. *Bulletin d'Information*, August 22, 1975.
223. Ibid.
224. "Discours de Samdech Norodom Sihanouk, Chef de l'Etat et President du Front Uni National du Kampuchea (Cambodge) a l'O.N.U.," October 6, 1975, p. 8.
225. Phnom Penh Domestic Service, January 9, 1976.
226. *Rice Bulletin*, November 1975, p. 2.
227. *Christian Science Monitor*, February 4, 1976; *New York Times*, January 21, 1976.
228. Vientiane Domestic Service, December 30, 1976.
229. Press conference held at the United Nations by Chief of the Delegation of Democratic Kampuchea to the United Nations Conference on the Law of the Sea, Mr. Thiounn Prasith, April 23, 1976.
230. Hsinhua News Service, April 15, 1976.
231. Phnom Penh Domestic Service, January 9, 1976.
232. Hsinhua News Service, April 15, 1976.
233. Ibid.
234. *Le Monde*, April 18-19, 1976.
235. Ibid.

236. Laura Summers, "Consolidating the Cambodian Revolution," *Current History*, December 1975, p. 220.

237. Delvert, *Le Paysan cambodgien*, p. 154.

238. Ibid., pp. 154-55.

239. Author's conversation with Mr. Thiounn Prasith, May 6, 1976.

240. Author's conversation with a Cambodian economist, May 1, 1976.

241. *Toronto Globe and Mail*, March 8, 1976.

242. *Washington Post*, April 28, 1976.

243. Private communication, December 15, 1975; copy in possession of the Indochina Resource Center.

244. Author's conversation with Mr. Thiounn Prasith, May 6, 1976.

245. Meyer, *Derrière le Sourire Khmer*, pp. 192-93.

246. Phnom Penh Domestic Service, July 8, 1975.

247. Delvert, *Le Paysan cambodgien*, pp. 331-32.

248. *Peking Review*, June 6, 1975; Phnom Penh Domestic Service, January 23, 1976; *Bulletin d'Information*, June 20, 1975; Hsinhua News Agency, May 16, 1976.

249. *Cambodia—News in Brief*, July 19, 1975.

250. United Nations General Assembly, Seventh Special Session, *Provisional Verbatim Record of the Two Thousand Three Hundred and Thirty-Fifth Meeting*, September 5, 1975, p. 7.

251. Phnom Penh Domestic Service, May 22, 1975.

252. "Economy and Efficiency of U.S. Programs in Laos and Cambodia," p. 114.

253. *Le Monde*, April 18-19, 1976.

254. Phnom Penh Domestic Service, July 9, December 7, 1975, and February 2, 1976; *Cambodia—News in Brief*, July 17, 1976.

255. *Le Monde*, April 18-19, 1976.

256. Author's conversation with a high-ranking Cambodian diplomat, November 15, 1975.

257. *Le Monde*, April 18-19, 1976.

258. Khieu Samphan, *The Economy of Cambodia*, p. 27.

259. Author's conversation with a Cambodian economist, May 1, 1976.

260. Author's conversation with Mr. Thiounn Prasith, May 6, 1976.

261. Exhibition of photographs from the magazine *Kampuchea*, New York City, April 17, 1976.

262. Hsinhua News Agency, April 15, 1976.

263. Author's conversation with a Cambodian economist, May 1, 1976.

264. Phnom Penh Domestic Service, April 15, 1976.

265. *Constitution du Kampuchea Democratique*, p. 3.

266. Press conference held at the United Nations by Chief of the Mission of the State of Democratic Kampuchea to the United Nations Conference on the Law of the Sea Mr. Thiounn Prasith, April 23, 1976.

267. Phnom Penh Domestic Service, July 11, 1975; *Bulletin d'Information*, September 19, 1975.

268. *Bulletin d'Information*, July 18, 1975; *Cambodia—News in Brief*, July 15, 1975.

269. *Bulletin d'Information*, July 4 and 20, 1975.

270. Ibid., May 23, 1975.

271. *Cambodia—News in Brief*, June 22, 1975.

272. Ibid., July 8, 1975; *A Heroic People*.

273. Exhibition of photographs from the magazine *Kampuchea*; author's conversation with a high-ranking Cambodian diplomat, April 17, 1976.

274. Hsinhua News Agency, April 17, 1976.

275. Phnom Penh Domestic Service, July 14, 1975.

276. Ibid., June 24, 1975.

277. Ibid., January 16, 1976.

278. Hsinhua News Agency, April 15, 1976.

279. Ibid.

280. Exhibition of photographs from the magazine *Kampuchea*.

281. Hsinhua News Agency, April 15, 1976.

282. Phnom Penh Domestic Service, May 27, 1975; *Bulletin d'Information*, July 18, 1975.

283. Exhibition of photographs from the magazine *Kampuchea*.

284. Phnom Penh Domestic Service, May 24, June 14, June 19, July 4, 1975; *Bulletin d'Information*, July 11, August 29, 1975.

285. Phnom Penh Domestic Service, May 14, May 23, May 25, June 1, 1975; *Cambodia—News in Brief*, June 14, 1975.

286. *Bulletin d'Information*, June 20, August 15, 1975.

287. Phnom Penh Domestic Service, June 14, 1975; Chandler, *The Land and People of Cambodia*, p. 20.

288. U.S. embassy, Phnom Penh, confidential report of Col. Robert L. Ventres, USAF, CMM USAFFG PAF Two USATSA Thai TM, July 4, 1974.

289. Phnom Penh Domestic Service, July 3, 1975.

290. *Area Handbook*, p. 264.

291. Phnom Penh Domestic Service, June 15, 1975.

292. Ibid.

293. Prud'homme, *L'Economie du Cambodge*, p. 79.

294. Phnom Penh Domestic Service. June 16, June 26, July 6, 1975; *Bulletin d'Information,* June 13, 1975.

295. IMF, "Report," p. 104.

296. *Bulletin d'Information*, June 13, 1975; *Cambodia—News in Brief*, June 19, 1975.

297. Phnom Penh Domestic Service, May 3, 23, 1975; *A Heroic People*.

298. Hsinhua News Agency, April 15, 1976.

299. Phnom Penh Domestic Service, February 24, 1976.

300. *Bulletin d'Information*, July 18, 1975.

301. "Communique of Mr. Hu Nim," p. 8; *Indochina Balance Sheet*, p. 4.

302. *Bulletin d'Information*, July 18, 1975.

303. Author's conversation with a high-ranking Cambodian diplomat, November 15, 1975.
304. Phnom Penh Domestic Service, May 30, 1975.